What People Ar
Arizona

"Here is a real fundamental basic crash course in Arizona law. Everything is taken care of in this book… You can find out more than you ever dreamed."

> —Pat McMahon, *The Pat McMahon Show*,
> KAZTV, Phoenix

"I love this book… it's a marvelous undertaking… simple to use; easy to understand… this book is so relevant… a tremendous amount of information."

> —John C. Scott, radio talk show host,
> KJLL, 1330 AM, Tucson

"Interpreting the legal jargon and navigating the various laws can be a daunting task for even a trained professional. That's why *Arizona Laws 101: A Handbook for Non-Lawyers* is so helpful. Written specifically for the layperson, 101 Arizona laws are interpreted and spelled out in a way that easily lays out the principles."

> —*BizAZ Magazine*

"Cutting through the Latin phrases and complex case law recitations that confuse laypeople, the softcover book explains the basics of our state's laws… [*Arizona Laws 101*] will allow you to be much better informed, and it's the sort of reference volume from which anyone can benefit."

> —*Tucson Lifestyle Magazine*

"[A] great service and resource for the citizens of Arizona."
> —Hon. Christopher Skelly, Maricopa County superior court judge (ret.)

"What an invaluable reference. You have done a real service for both non-lawyers and lawyers."
> —Merton E. Marks, Esq., arbitrator and mediator

"It is important to have this book if you moved here from somewhere else...it gives you guidelines, a place to go."
> —*AM Arizona*, KAZ-TV, Prescott

"This is a great reference point for people learning on the fly."
> —*Good Morning Tucson*, KGUN, Tucson

"This book may answer a lot of your questions...good information."
> —*Arizona Midday*, KPNX, Phoenix

"A tool that will help answer the most common legal questions you may have."
> —*Arizona Morning*, KSAZ Fox, Phoenix

"You did good work on this...it's got everything in it."
> —*Good Morning Arizona*, KTVK, Phoenix

Estate Planning in Arizona

Estate Planning in Arizona

What You Need to Know

A handbook for those interested in
wealth preservation, family protection,
and succession planning

Donald A. Loose
Attorney at Law

Estate Planning in Arizona: What You Need to Know

Published by Wheatmark®
610 East Delano Street, Suite 104
Tucson, Arizona 85705 U.S.A.
www.wheatmark.com

Publisher's Cataloging-In-Publication Data
(Prepared by The Donohue Group, Inc.)

Loose, Donald A.
  Estate planning in Arizona : what you need to know : a handbook for those interested in wealth preservation, family protection, and succession planning / Donald A. Loose.

   p. ; cm.

   ISBN: 978-1-60494-000-8

1. Estate planning—Arizona—Popular works. 2. Probate law and practice—Arizona—Popular works. 3. Finance, Personal—Arizona—Popular works. I. Title.

KF750 .L66 2008
332.024/016/09791   2007940104

To my sons, John and Grant

Contents

Part Three: Powers of Attorney and Medical Directives

Part Four: Property and Gifts

Appendixes

Introduction

The information contained in this book is intended to assist those interested in estate planning by providing what they need to know to accomplish their goals. The goals often include paying the least amount of estate and gift taxes and avoiding probate. That having been said, this book does not substitute for legal advice, and a qualified attorney should always be consulted regarding estate planning matters.

This book is divided into five distinct but related parts: wills and trusts, probate, powers of attorney and medical directives, property and gifts, and forms. The parts together constitute a primer on estate planning. The parts separately cover the topics described. The reader is thus free to pick and choose among the various topics and forms.

The primary goal of this book is to make a complex subject just a little bit simpler. The more that you know about estate planning, the better able you will be to assist counsel in preparing an estate plan to accomplish *your* goals.

About the Author

DONALD LOOSE is the founder and managing partner of Loose, Brown & Associates, P.C. The firm, with offices in Phoenix and Tucson, provides legal services and representation to individuals and businesses throughout Arizona. Don's practice is  concentrated in the areas of business, litigation, and estates. In the more than twenty-five years that Don has practiced law in Arizona, he has counseled untold numbers of clients on wealth preservation, family protection, and succession planning issues. This is Don's second book. His first book, *Arizona Laws 101: A Handbook for Non-Lawyers*, was first published in 2005 and won an Arizona Book Award. Don is a frequent guest on television and radio talk shows where he is invited to discuss legal issues and events.

Acknowledgment

I would like to gratefully acknowledge the contributions made by Melina Greenberg in the creation of this book. Melina is a talented and enthusiastic young lawyer with whom I have had the pleasure of working during the past two years. Melina wrote several of the draft chapters, researched topics and legal issues, and located the forms for the appendixes. She also proofread the preliminary draft to check for substantive and grammatical errors, and worked with my editor and me on the cover design. Without Melina's invaluable assistance, this book would be less than it is. I am indebted to her for her contributions.

PART ONE

Wills and Trusts

Wills

A will is a legal declaration of a person's intention, which he wills to be performed after his death. No particular form of will is required, so long as there has been compliance with the legal requirements as discussed below. The law of wills differs from state to state. This chapter is based entirely on Arizona law.

Any person eighteen years or older and of "sound mind" may execute a will. A person who executes a will is called a "testator." The law does not require any residence or citizenship so that nonresidents of Arizona and aliens may make valid wills in Arizona.

There are many ways that property may be disposed of after death: (a) under a will or living trust, (b) pursuant to joint tenancy and community property survivorship provisions, (c) by "pay on death" clauses and insurance contract designations, and (d) by informal lists (for tangible personal property such as jewelry and furniture). The most common way for property to be disposed of after death is under a will, although living trusts are becoming more popular and, in many cases, have the important benefit of avoiding taxes and probate. (Living trusts and other forms of property disposition are discussed in subsequent chapters.)

Legal Requirements

A will must be signed by the testator or by someone at his direction and in his conscious presence. A person may sign by making a mark ("X") if illiterate or incapacitated. Two attesting witnesses must sign the will. Interestingly, there is no requirement that the witnesses sign in the presence of the testator or each other, although most often all three persons (the testator and two witnesses) sign the will at the same time in each other's presence.

Under Arizona law, a beneficiary under the will may act as a witness. The law in many other states is different. Earlier Arizona law invalidated the whole will if a beneficiary acted as a witness.

Foreign wills do not necessarily have to be redone in Arizona to be valid. A written will is valid if it is executed in compliance with the law of the state or country in which it is executed. Therefore, a will that was valid when it was executed outside the state of Arizona is valid in Arizona, regardless of where it was executed or whether it meets Arizona's requirements for execution.

A will may be made "self-proved" either at the time of the original execution or later. A self-proved will contains an acknowledgment by the testator and affidavit of the witnesses before a notary public. The advantage of a self-proved will is greatest in a will contest. If a self-proved will is contested in court, the formalities of proper execution are conclusively presumed.

Holographic and Oral Wills

A "holographic will" is a will that is in the testator's handwriting and not witnessed. Holographic wills are valid in Arizona if the signature and material provisions are in the handwriting of the testator. A testator can create a valid holographic will by using a preprinted form, as long as the form is signed, and the designation of beneficiaries and the estate appointment are in the testator's own handwriting. A holographic will does not need to be dated.

Arizona formerly allowed oral wills if made in the testator's last illness before three witnesses, but that statute has been repealed. An oral will is no longer valid.

Separate Writing for Tangible Personal Property

The law allows a separate writing to dispose of items of *tangible personal property*. Tangible personal property is property which may be felt or touched, such as a chair, a computer, or a watch. The purpose of this provision is to allow a testator to prepare a separate list of things, such as furniture, household goods, jewelry, antiques, pictures, guns, and other personal effects, that the testator wants distributed to relatives and friends. The list does not have to comply with the normal formalities for execution (discussed earlier), but it must be referred to in a properly executed will and must be in the handwriting of the testator and signed by him. The list can be made up after the execution of the will and changed from time to time if the testator so wishes. This is a particularly useful provision if the testator has not thought through his wishes with respect to these items at the time he executes his will, if his possessions are likely to change, or if he may want to change the list later.

Although there is no limit on the value of the tangible personal property that can be disposed of by such a list, it would be unwise to use the list as a means of passing valuable jewelry, antiques, collections, paintings, vehicles, or the like. These items should be specifically disposed of by the will and the list used only for items of relatively small value. It should be noted that a testator may execute an attested will and later execute in his own handwriting a document disposing of any kind of property he wishes. In other words, a valid holographic will can revoke the provisions of the attested will, and the holographic will is not limited to tangible personal property.

Personal Representative

A testator may nominate a personal representative in his will. A personal representative (formerly known as an executor) administers the will following the testator's death. Any person eighteen years of age or older is qualified to serve as a personal representative unless the court finds that person to be unsuitable. A person who is incompetent, for example, would be unsuitable to serve as personal representative. A corporation or other legal entity may also serve as a personal representative. Neither Arizona residence nor United States citizenship is required for a personal representative. Of course, consent of the person or institution to be named should be secured prior to completing the will to assure that the nominee will serve.

The testator may request that the personal representative serve without bond. A bond is a form of security that in most cases takes the form of an insurance policy. It protects the beneficiaries in case the personal representative fails to properly perform his duties. In the absence of a waiver of bond in the will, the court may require a bond. Qualified trust companies and banks are not required to post bonds, however.

Once appointed by the court, the powers of the personal representative are very broad and comprehensive. Generally, no further court authorization or approval is required for the personal representative to exercise those powers.

A personal representative is entitled to reasonable compensation for his services, and the will may specify the amount of the fee.

Guardian for Minor Children

A testator can also nominate a guardian for minor children in a validly executed will. (For a discussion regarding guardians, please refer to that chapter in part four.) A guardian is a person who is generally responsible for the health, welfare, and safety of a minor. It is a good practice for the parent of a minor child to nominate a guardian for the child in the event the other parent predeceases the testator or is not able to care for the child after the testator's death. It should be noted, however, that a minor fourteen years of age or over may object to the appointment of the guardian nominated in the will.

Revocation

Two distinguishing characteristics of a will are that it is cancelable (revocable) prior to death and that it takes effect only at death. A testator may cancel a will in whole or in part by executing a subsequent will that revokes the previous will or part expressly or by inconsistency or by performing a "revocatory act." Burning, tearing, canceling, obliterating, or destroying the will or any part of it with the intent to revoke it will be sufficient. The physical act must be accompanied by the present intent to revoke. The requisite physical act can even be performed by a third person if directed by the testator to be done in his presence.

A will may also be revoked by operation of law. A divorce or annulment revokes the provisions in a will in favor of the ex-spouse and his or her relatives. Revocation will also occur in cases where there is a felonious and intentional killing of the testator.

If a testator marries after executing the will and does not provide for his or her spouse, the surviving spouse is entitled to a share equal to the share he or she would have received had the decedent died without a will. This is another situation in which a will is changed by operation of law and not by any act of the testator.

Benefits of Having a Will

Irrespective of the primary means by which assets are disposed of at the time of death (e.g., will, living trust, joint tenancy, etc.), a validly executed will has a place in almost every estate plan. If the will is the instrument by which all or part of the assets will be disposed of, then its importance is primary in the estate plan. However, even in a case where a living trust or some other will-substitute is used to dispose of property, a will is still valuable because it enables the testator to use a separate writing for tangible personal property, to give funeral and burial directions, and to nominate a guardian for minor children. In cases where a living trust has been prepared, a will ensures that any assets outside the trust at the testator's death are poured over to the trust.

Ten Common Misconceptions about Wills

1. **If I don't have a will, my property will go to the state.** False. If you don't have a will, your property will go to your heirs under the law of descent and distribution in Arizona. Your property will go to the state only if you die without a will *and* you have no living relative to inherit it.

2. **If I have a will, all of my property will automatically pass under it.** False. Some or all of your property may pass outside your will by reason of survivorship provisions, joint title, pay-on-death clauses, and beneficiary designations in deeds and contracts. For instance, life insurance proceeds will be payable to the beneficiaries that you have designated in the insurance contract, regardless of the terms of your will.

3. **The will that I executed before I moved to Arizona is invalid.** False. If your will was valid in the state or country in which it was executed, it is valid in Arizona. (Yet it is a

good idea to update your will in your new state.)

4. **I have to execute a living trust to avoid taxes on my estate.** False. Most estates will *not* be subject to taxation with or without a living trust. In 2008, up to $2,000,000 is exempt from estate taxes (assuming no lifetime transfers—see Unified Credit Exemption Amounts in appendix A). The unified credit exemption is scheduled to increase to $3,500,000 in 2009 before repeal in 2010. If you are married, you can leave an unlimited amount to your spouse without payment of any estate taxes.

5. **If I execute a will, my estate will be subjected to costly attorney fees and probate charges when I die.** False. It is not inherently expensive to probate a will in Arizona. An informal and inexpensive probate process is available in most cases. There are no separate probate fees other than a small filing fee to start the case.

6. **It is always less expensive to leave my property under a living trust than a will.** False. In some cases it is actually more expensive to create a living trust than to informally probate an estate. It depends on the nature and value of your assets.

7. **If I execute a will, I will be unable to create a trust for my children.** False. One or more

trusts can be created in a will. These are known as "testamentary trusts," and they take effect upon the death of the person executing the will (the "testator"). By use of a testamentary trust, you can set aside money or property for the future benefit of your children. The testamentary trust will be administered by the trustee you appoint in your will.

8. **If my estate is probated under a will, my assets will be tied up for years in the courts.** False. Informal probate can be started almost immediately after your death, allows the personal representative immediate access to your assets, and, in most cases, can be completed in nine months or less.

9. **My will must be filed after it is executed.** False. In Arizona, there is no provision for the filing of a will until after the death of the testator. The original stays with the testator after execution.

10. **It is better to keep my will in a safe deposit box than at home.** False. Accessing a safe deposit box is often difficult and time consuming after the death of the person renting the box. A better place to keep your will is at home with your other important papers, where family members can easily access it.

Living Trusts

Any discussion about living trusts should properly start with a definition of the term. A living trust is a legal entity that is created and holds title to assets during the life of the person who places assets inside the trust. That person is known as the "settlor."

The trust is created by executing a trust agreement and transferring the settlor's assets to the trust. The trust holds title to the assets. However, even though the settlor relinquishes *title* to the assets, the settlor still retains *control* of those assets. A trustee appointed by the settlor manages the trust assets. In most cases, the settlor is also the initial trustee. As the trustee of the trust, the settlor continues to have the same power to buy, sell, transfer, and otherwise control the trust assets.

Illustration #1: John executes a trust agreement, thereby creating a living trust. John then transfers title to his house to himself, *as the trustee of his trust*. John is both the settlor and the initial trustee in this example. Although the trust now holds title to John's house, John still retains control of it.

The trust is *revocable*, which means that it can be modified or terminated by the settlor for as long as the settlor is alive and competent to make a contract. In some sophisticated estate plans, it may be desirable to create one or more *irrevocable* trusts, but irrevocable trusts are beyond the scope of this chapter.

Parties to a Trust

As we saw in Illustration #1, a person who creates a revocable trust may serve different functions simultaneously. The settlor is the person who creates the trust. (The Internal Revenue Service refers to the settlor as the grantor and to the trust as a grantor's trust.)

The *trustee* is the person who handles the administration of the trust. When a trust is first created, the trustee is usually the same person as the settlor. When a married couple creates a trust, both spouses usually serve as the trustees.

The *surviving trustee* is the person who continues to manage the trust after one of the original trustees has died. The surviving spouse is typically the primary *beneficiary* as well as the surviving trustee. A *successor trustee* is a person or entity that is named to succeed the surviving trustee upon death or incompetence. The successor trustee has the same powers as the original trustees.

Assets

For a trust to be effective in avoiding probate and minimizing taxation, all of the settlor's assets must be placed inside the trust. Assets may include bank accounts, real estate, and motor vehicles. The process involves simply turning the title to the assets over to the trust. The person who controls the assets does not change; only the title to the assets does.

Except for real estate deeds, transferring assets into the trust should have no cost. The settlor is the person who (with the assistance of counsel where necessary) places the assets into the trust and is the same person who has the right to also transfer those assets from the trust. Assets acquired after the trust is created should also be titled in the name of the trust.

Illustration #2: John sells his house after it has been transferred into the trust, and he buys another. The new house should also be titled in the name of the trust.

Because the settlor owns nothing in his name (all of the assets were placed in the trust), there is nothing to probate upon his death. If the settlor is married, the surviving spouse typically becomes the surviving trustee and, as such, continues to have the same power to buy, sell, or transfer the assets. Upon the death of the surviving spouse, the same situation applies as before. Since no assets were in the name of the deceased, there is nothing to probate. The trust document will identify who is to act as the successor trustee upon the death of surviving spouse.

Types of Trusts

The trust document can take one of several basic forms. The two basic forms that will be discussed in this chapter are the A Trust and the

A-B Trust. These are the most common. There are other forms of trusts (such as the A-B-C Trust), but they are best left to be explained by estate-planning counsel retained for that purpose.

One important reason for having a trust is to avoid paying unnecessary estate taxes. The form that best suits a particular situation will depend on the person's marital status, the value of the estate, and the potential distribution desired for the heirs.

The A Trust can be used for single persons or married couples but must always be used when only one person is involved. (The preceding illustrations assumed an A Trust.) For estates valued at less than $2,000,000 in 2008, the entire estate will be passed down to the heirs without estate taxes. For estates valued at more than that amount, estate tax will be due. (The $2,000,000 unified credit exemption amount, referenced in the second to last sentence, increases to $3,500,000 in 2009, before repeal in 2010. For a table of unified credit exemption amounts, see appendix A.)

The A-B Trust is generally used when two people are involved in the trust, whether they are married or unmarried. Couples whose combined estate now exceeds $2,000,000 should consider the A-B Trust in order to take advantage of the unified credit exemption. Upon the death of one person, generally half of the assets will flow down into the B (or decedent's) Trust, and the other half of the assets will be passed down to the survivor in the A (or survivor's) Trust. The entire estate will remain available to be used by the survivor, subject to certain restrictions imposed by the IRS.

Illustration #3: John and Mary, a married couple, create an A-B Trust. Their combined estate is worth $3,000,000. Assuming John dies, half of the assets, worth $1,500,000, flow down into the B (or decedent's) Trust, and the other half of the assets, also worth $1,500,000, pass down to Mary in the A (or survivor's) Trust. The entire estate will remain available to be used by Mary, subject to the restrictions discussed in the following paragraph. There will be no estate tax owed as a result of John's death.

In most revocable trusts, the surviving spouse is named as the beneficiary of the B Trust (as in the above illustration) and, accordingly, has the right to all of the income of the B Trust; the right to use the principal in the B Trust for certain enumerated purposes; and the right to spend $5,000 (or 5 percent of the assets—whichever is greater) in the B Trust each year, for any reason. The surviving spouse retains absolute control over the assets in the A Trust.

As shown, the use of a revocable trust in an estate plan can avoid probate and eliminate or reduce estate tax in some cases. Every person owning assets, regardless of the assets' value, should consult estate-planning counsel to consider whether a living trust is right for him or her.

Special-Purpose Trusts

A trust is a legal entity that is created and holds title to assets during the life of the person who places assets inside the trust. The use of a special trust may be desirable to meet the unique challenges presented by a blended-family situation (where the family structure has changed because of divorce, separation, or remarriage) or to avoid payment of estate taxes. Here, we examine two common forms of special trusts.

» *Qualified Terminable Interest Property (QTIP) Trust.* The QTIP trust is often used when one spouse has remarried. It is a special trust that lets the maker of the trust, called the settlor, use the unlimited marriage deduction, provide for her spouse after her death, and defer potential estate taxes until the second death while retaining ultimate control over the distribution of her property. In using a QTIP trust, a certain portion of the settlor's assets is transferred upon death into a trust that pays income (and potentially principal) to the settlor's spouse for his lifetime. At the spouse's death, the principal passes to the beneficiaries that the settlor has designated.

» *Irrevocable Life Insurance Trust (ILIT)*. The ILIT trust allows an insurance policy to be held in a trust, so that it will not be included in the settlor's taxable estate. In order for the settlor to receive full tax advantages offered by an ILIT, she cannot name herself or her spouse as the trustee. Currently, an individual can contribute $12,000 annually ($24,000 if married) per beneficiary to pay the premiums on the life insurance policy held in the trust. Upon the death of the settlor, or the settlor and spouse, the life insurance policy's proceeds are paid to the trust. The trustee then distributes that money to the beneficiaries as outlined by the terms of the trust.

The use of any trust for estate planning purposes ultimately will depend on a variety of factors, including the size and complexity of the estate, the need to avoid taxes, and the settlor's desire to distribute assets outright or in trust. As shown above, the use of a special trust may help further the settlor's specific goals and objectives.

Funding a Trust

Creating a trust is a significant step toward financial security for many people. When a person takes this step, he accepts added responsibility. As trustee, he will initially be concerned with the funding of his trust. In most circumstances, a revocable trust will be created primarily for tax and estate planning purposes. A secondary benefit of a revocable trust is that the estate will not have to be probated if the settlor (the person creating the trust) transfers all of his assets into the name of the trust.

Funding the trust is critical. The trustee of a trust works only with assets that have been transferred or funded to him in the name of the trust. To the extent that any of the assets in the settlor's name are not funded to the trustee prior to his death, they may be subject to a probate administration.

Funding a Trust

After creating the trust, it is necessary to fund it by identifying assets that the settlor desires to make a part of the trust. Usually, funding a trust involves changing the legal ownership of property from the settlor's name to the trustee's name.

Property placed in the trust can be held in the trust's name:

John Doe and Jane Doe, as Trustees of the Doe Family Trust, dated _____.

The following discussion can serve as a funding checklist.

✓ Home and Other Real Estate

Including a home and other real estate in the trust requires an attorney to draw up a new deed and have it recorded.

Under Arizona law, a deed to real estate which indicates that a trust owns the real estate must disclose the beneficial owners of the real estate. The beneficial owners of real estate held in trust are the beneficiaries of the trust. In nearly all cases, the beneficiaries of the trust are also the settlors. So long as the deed to the real estate discloses the beneficial owners, it is not necessary to also record the actual trust documents.

Real estate located outside the state of Arizona may pose a special problem, because in many cases a corporate trustee (such as a bank) or successor trustee from Arizona will not be empowered to act in the state in which the real estate is located. This may preclude a conveyance to the trustee and necessitate use of a nominee partnership. A nominee partnership is created for the sole purpose of holding the title to trust assets. If a nominee partnership is used, a nominee partnership agreement should be prepared in addition to the trust agreement.

Any interest in real estate less than absolute ownership, such as an agreement of sale or a lessee's interest, may also be assigned to the trust. The terms of the agreement of sale, lease, or other relevant document should be reviewed by an attorney to assure that assignment is permitted.

✓ Stocks and Bonds

Stocks and bonds, including all registered securities, must be put in the trust's name. A stockbroker or banker can assist the trustee. After completing the necessary documents, a broker or banker arranges to forward the certificates to the transfer agent. The transfer agent issues new certificates in the name of the trust, as discussed above.

A trustee may experience delays in receiving new certificates, because of the need for security and the transfer agent's workload. If significant transfers of registered securities are anticipated and speed of transfer is critical, it may be preferable to create a separate nominee partnership to hold title to the securities.

Alternatively, if there is considerable trading activity, securities may be held in the broker's street name account (i.e., the broker will retain the securities in its name). This is the simplest approach only when the trust maintains sufficient trading activity. It should be noted that stock held in a street name account can be used by the stock broker for its own use, thus exposing the settlor's assets to greater liability. For this reason alone, a settlor may wish to avoid the use of a street name account.

Unregistered securities (i.e., those in bearer form) present no particular transfer problems, and obviously there are no registration problems. A short form of assignment from the settlor to the trustee of the trust should be executed. For example:

> The undersigned hereby assigns all right, title, and interest in and to the following securities to John Doe and Jane Doe, as Trustees of the Doe Family Trust, dated
> _____.

This assignment should describe the property with some specificity to adequately evidence the settlor's intent that it be considered a trust asset.

If the settlor has Series EE Bonds or Series HH Bonds and desires to retain them, he can submit an application to the Federal Reserve Board, 409 West Olympic, Los Angeles, California 80015, on the Bureau's Form PD 1851, for a reissuance of each bond in the trustee's name. Each new bond bears the original issue date, and no income tax consequences result.

✓ Tangible Personal Property

Because tangible personal property, such as household furniture and furnishings, jewelry, antiques, artwork, and the like, is without any recognized documentation of title, funding of this property is done by using a simple assignment from the settlor to the trustee (in the same manner utilized in funding bearer securities). However, in that tangible personal property changes constantly and continuous additional assignments would be impractical, the initial assignment should cover "any and all tangible personal property now owned or hereafter acquired."

✓ Bank Accounts

Generally, the simplest method in handling checking and savings accounts is to open new accounts in the trust's name:

> John Doe and Jane Doe, as Trustees of the
> Doe Family Trust, dated _____.

This statement is the formal registration for these accounts as trust accounts. It must be identified as that when recorded on the signature card. Trust identification does not have to appear on checks, savings statements, or passbooks, but it must appear on the financial institution's records.

Savings certificates and other time deposits are handled in the same way.

✓ Life Insurance

Whether or not life insurance should be funded to the trust depends on a variety of circumstances, which are different for every person. If a settlor wants his life insurance in the trust, he must change the beneficiary to the trust. For example:

The then-acting Trustee or Trustees of the Doe Family Trust dated _____.

It is recommended that the settlor check with his insurance agent for guidance as to whether or not his life insurance should be funded to his trust. If a policy has cash value, it may be necessary to change both its ownership and the beneficiary designation.

✓ Retirement Benefits

The vested portion of retirement benefits is made payable to the trustee in the same manner as life insurance. However, careful planning and analysis is necessary before retirement benefits are funded to a trust.

If the settlor has his own pension or profit sharing plan, an attorney can make the necessary designation. To guarantee any nontaxable status which these benefits might have, care should be taken to assure that the trust agreement insulates these benefits from claims and expenses in the settlor's estate. There are two methods to name the trust as recipient of retirement benefits, depending upon the terms of the pension trust. The trust is named either in the insurance policy, if one exists, or by completing a document called a Designation of Beneficiary Form.

Generally, it is advisable for a person to name his spouse as the first beneficiary of a retirement benefit, including an Individual Retirement Account (IRA).

✓ Closely Held or "Family" Corporations and Partnerships

Transferring business interests into a trust is a complex situation with many variables to consider. It is recommended that the settlor check with an attorney to determine the best course of action.

✓ Miscellaneous Items

As one might surmise, there are many other types of assets not discussed in this chapter. If a person has assets of significant value and he wants to put them into the trust, he should contact an attorney for suggestions to help him achieve his goal.

Protecting Trust Assets and Identifying the Trust for Tax Purposes

Protecting Trust Assets

Once the trust agreement has been signed and assets have been transferred to the trust, the trust agreement is fully operative as to those assets. At this point, there are certain basic steps that the trustee should take.

If an asset should be covered by insurance, it should be so protected after it has been transferred to the trust. If insurance is already covering a trust asset, the insurance policy should be revised to add the trustee as named insured on the policy. This can usually be done at no additional cost. When personal property, an automobile, or a residence is transferred to the trust, the trustee should make sure that the particular asset is covered by insurance and that the trustee is a named insured.

If the trust holds certificates of title, stock certificates, or negotiable instruments, those valuable documents should be placed in a safe deposit box. If the safe deposit box holds only trust assets and is in the name of the trustee, there will be no problem in identifying bearer bonds or unregistered securities as trust assets. In addition, by holding the box in the name of the trustee (as opposed to in the settlor's name alone), there will be someone with immediate authority to enter the safe deposit box upon the settlor's death or disability.

Identifying the Trust for Tax Purposes

The trust is a separate entity and an identifying number (the settlor's social security number) is required for it for income tax purposes. The settlor's social security number should be given to banks, corporations, and others who pay interest or dividend income to the trust. The IRS formerly required a separate identifying number, but this practice has been stopped in favor of using the settlor's social security number.

The trustee of a trust is not required to file a fiduciary income tax return. If the trust is a fully revocable trust, all income will be reported directly on the settlor's individual tax return (IRS Form 1040). Upon the settlor's death, a separate tax identification number will be necessary for any trust that is thereby created and funded (e.g., the B Trust).

Administering the Trust

The trustee is the legal owner of the trust assets. If more than one trustee is acting, the trustees own the trust assets with survivorship rights similar to those of joint tenants. Property held in the name of trustees will pass to the surviving trustee and any successor trustee upon the death of a trustee. If more than one trustee is acting, the trustees must act together unless otherwise expressly provided by the trust agreement. A trustee is not acting as the agent of the beneficiaries of the trust. A trustee's actions are her own and she is responsible for them.

Of critical importance in the creation of a trust is the trust agreement. The trust agreement instructs the trustee how to manage, administer, and dispose of the assets which are transferred to the trust. These guidelines are directed primarily at the revocable trust situation, where the trust was created by the settlor primarily to avoid probate, and the settlor is the trustee or co-trustee (often with another family member) and is also the primary beneficiary during her lifetime. As settlor and trustee of this type of trust, the settlor's wishes as to the management and disposition of the trust assets will control during her lifetime. Nevertheless, there are certain basic obligations, such as the duties to keep records and to segregate trust property and to file any required tax returns. The exercise of these functions reflects the fact that the settlor intends the assets to be part of a trust arrangement under which other parties have interests.

The settlor should keep good financial records, whether her investments are held in her name or in trust. If the settlor has good records, the trust should not increase her workload. Even where the settlor is the trustee of a trust for her own benefit, a trust cannot be set up and funded and then forgotten.

The trustee has a responsibility to keep accurate records concerning the trust assets. She should set up books (with the help of an accountant, if necessary) to identify (1) income received, (2) income paid out, (3) additions to principal, (4) deductions from principal, (5) principal on hand, and (6) changes in trust investments. All transactions involving trust assets should be carefully documented. When records are originally set up, the cost basis of all assets transferred to the trust should be determined. It is much easier to obtain this information while the settlor is alive and her records available than to try to track down the information when the assets are sold or otherwise transferred. In addition, to satisfying the trustee's legal responsibilities, accurate books and records will make the successor trustee's job much easier.

Powers of a Trustee

During the term of the trust, the trustee has the power to perform, without court authorization, every act which a prudent person dealing with the property of another would perform for the purposes of the trust. Under Arizona law, a trustee has the power to do all of the following:

» Collect, hold, and retain trust assets received from the settlor until, in the judgment of the trustee, disposition of the assets should be made. (The assets may be retained even though they include an asset in which the trustee is personally interested.)

» Receive additions to the assets of the trust.

» Continue or participate in the operation of any business or other enterprise and to effect incorporation, dissolution, or other change in the form of the organization of the business or enterprise.

» Acquire an undivided interest in a trust asset

in which the trustee, in any trust capacity, holds an undivided interest.

» Invest and reinvest trust assets in accordance with the provisions of the trust or as provided by law.

» Deposit trust funds in a bank or savings and loan association, including a bank or savings and loan association operated by the trustee.

» Acquire or dispose of an asset, for cash or on credit, at public or private sale, to manage, develop, improve, exchange, partition, change the character of, or abandon a trust asset or any interest in a trust asset and to encumber, mortgage, or pledge a trust asset for a term within or extending beyond the term of the trust, in connection with the exercise of any power vested in the trustee.

» Make ordinary or extraordinary repairs or alternations in buildings or other structures, to demolish any improvements, and to raze existing or erect new party walls or buildings.

» Subdivide, develop, or dedicate land to public use; to make or obtain the vacation of plats and adjust boundaries; to adjust differences in valuation on exchange or partition by giving or receiving consideration or to dedicate easements to public use without consideration.

» Enter for any purpose into a lease as lessor or lessee with or without the option to purchase or renew for a term within or extending beyond the term of the trust.

» Enter into a lease or arrangement for exploration and removal of minerals or other natural resources or enter into a pooling or unitization agreement.

» Grant an option involving disposition of a trust asset or to take an option for the acquisition of any asset.

» Vote a security in person or by general or limited proxy.

» Pay assessments and any other amounts chargeable or accruing against or on account of securities.

» Sell or exercise stock subscription or conversion rights or to consent, directly or through a committee or other agent, to the reorganization, consolidation, merger, dissolution, or liquidation of a corporation or other business enterprise.

» Hold a security in the name of a nominee or in other form without disclosure of the trust, so that title to the security may pass by delivery, but the trustee is liable for any act of the nominee in connection with the stock so held.

» Insure the assets of the trust against damage or loss and the trustee against liability with respect to third persons.

» Borrow money (to be repaid from trust assets or otherwise); to advance money for the protection of the trust and for all expenses, losses, and liabilities sustained in the administration of the trust or because of the holding or ownership of any trust assets, for which advances with any interest the trustee has a lien on the trust assets as against the beneficiary.

» Pay or contest any claim; to settle a claim by or against the trust by compromise, arbitration, or otherwise; and to release, in whole or in part, any claim belonging to the trust to the extent that the claim is uncollectible.

» Pay taxes, assessments, compensation of the trustee and other expenses incurred in the collection, care, administration and protection of the trust.

» Allocate items of income or expense to either trust income or principal.

» Pay any sum distributable to a beneficiary under legal disability, without liability to the trustee, by paying the sum to the beneficiary or by paying the sum for the use of the beneficiary either to a legal representative appointed by the court or, if none, to a relative.

» Effect distribution of property and money in divided or undivided interests and to adjust resulting differences in valuation.

» Employ persons, including attorneys, auditors, investment advisors, or agents, even if they are associated with the trustee, to advise or assist the trustee in the performance of his administrative duties; to act without independent investigation on their recommendations; and, instead of acting personally, to employ one or more agents to perform any act of administration, whether or not discretionary.

» Prosecute or defend actions, claims, or proceedings for the protection of trust assets and of the trustee in the performance of his duties.

» Execute and deliver all instruments which will accomplish or facilitate the exercise of the powers vested in the trustee.

If the trust agreement or a court order requires or authorizes investment in United States government obligations, a trustee may invest in these obligations either directly or in the form of securities or other interests in any open-end or closed-end management type investment company or investment trust, if certain conditions are met. The trustee should consult an attorney if he has any questions about investing in an investment company or investment trust.

Powers not Transferable

A trustee cannot transfer his office to another or delegate the entire administration of the trust to a co-trustee or another.

Court-Approved Transactions

A court, on petition of the trustee or a beneficiary, may relieve the trustee from any restrictions on his power that would otherwise be placed on him by the trust or by statute. If the duty of the trustee and his individual interest (or his interest as trustee of another trust) conflict in the exercise of a trust power, the power generally may be exercised only by court authorization.

Powers by Joint Trustees

Any power vested in three or more trustees may be exercised by a majority, but a trustee who has not joined in exercising a power is not liable to the beneficiaries or to others for the consequences of the exercise. A dissenting trustee is not liable for the consequences of an act in which she joins at the direction of the majority of the trustees, if she expressed her dissent in writing to any of her co-trustees at or before the time of the joinder.

If two or more trustees are appointed to perform a trust and if any of them is unable or refuses to accept the appointment (or, after having accepted, ceases to be a trustee) the surviving or remaining trustees must perform the trust and succeed to all the powers, duties and discretionary authority given to the trustees jointly.

The law does not excuse a co-trustee from liability for failure either to participate in the administration of the trust or to attempt to prevent a breach of trust.

Third Persons Dealing With Trustee

A third person dealing with a trustee or assisting a trustee in the conduct of a transaction, may assume the existence of trust powers and their proper exercise by the trustee without inquiry. The third person is not bound to inquire whether the trustee has power to act or is properly exercising the power. A third person, without actual knowledge that the trustee is exceeding his powers or improperly exercising them, is fully protected in dealing with the trustee as if the trustee possessed and properly exercised the powers he purports to exercise. Finally, a third person is not bound to assure the proper application of trust assets paid or delivered to the trustee.

Duties of a Trustee

The general duty of a trustee is to administer the trust expeditiously for the benefit of the beneficiaries. The trustee must observe the standard in dealing with the trust assets that would be observed by a "prudent man" dealing with the property of another. If the trustee has special skills or is named trustee on the basis of representations of special skills or expertise, she is under a duty to use those skills.

The duties of a trustee are discussed in greater detail below.

Duty to Inform

The trustee must keep the beneficiaries of the trust reasonably informed of the trust and its administration. Additionally, within thirty days after her acceptance of the trust, the trustee must inform the beneficiaries currently entitled to receive income, of the trustee's name and address in writing. Upon reasonable request, the trustee must provide a beneficiary with a copy of the terms of the trust which describe or affect the beneficiary's interest and with relevant information about the assets of the trust and the particulars relating to the administration. Upon reasonable request, a beneficiary is entitled to a statement of the accounts of the trust annually and on termination of the trust or change of the trustee.

Duty to Provide Bond

A trustee need not provide bond to secure performance of her duties unless: (1) required by the terms of the trust, (2) reasonably requested by a beneficiary, or (3) found by the court to be necessary to protect the interests of the beneficiaries who are not able to protect themselves and whose interests otherwise are not adequately represented. On petition of the trustee or other interested person, the court may excuse a requirement of bond, reduce the amount of the bond, release the surety, or permit the substitution of another bond with the same or different sureties. If bond is required, it must be filed in the court of the county where the trust has its principal place of administration or in another appropriate court.

Appropriate Place of Administration

A trustee is under a continuing duty to administer the trust at a place appropriate to the purposes of the trust and to its sound, efficient management. If the principal place of administration becomes inappropriate for any reason, the court may enter an order furthering efficient administration and the interests of beneficiaries, including, if appropriate, removal of the trustee and appointment of a trustee in another state.

Trust provisions relating to the place of administration and to changes in the place of administration or of trustee control should govern, unless compliance would be contrary to efficient administration or the purposes of the trust. Views of adult beneficiaries should be given weight in determining the suitability of the trustee and the place of administration.

Liability to Third Parties

Unless otherwise provided in the contract, or unless she fails to reveal her representative capacity and identify the trust estate in the contract, a trustee is not personally liable on contracts properly entered into in her fiduciary capacity in the course of administration of the trust estate.

A trustee is, however, personally liable for obligations arising from ownership or control of property of the trust estate or for torts committed in the course of administration of the trust estate, if she is personally at fault.

Claims based on contracts entered into by a trustee in her fiduciary capacity, on obligations arising from ownership or control of the trust estate, or on torts committed in the course of trust administration, may be asserted against the trust estate by proceeding against the trustee in her fiduciary capacity, whether or not the trustee is personally liable.

Proceedings against Trustee

A claim for breach of trust by a beneficiary must be asserted no later than six months from the date she receives a statement fully disclosing the trust matter and shows termination of the trust relationship between the trustee and the beneficiary. In any event, a trustee who has issued a final account or statement received by the beneficiary and has informed the beneficiary of the location and availability of records for her examination is protected after three years. A beneficiary is deemed to have received a final account or statement if, being an adult, it is received by her personally or if, being a minor or disabled person, it is received by her representative.

Investments in Name of Nominee

Any state or national bank or title insurance company, when acting in Arizona as a fiduciary, may cause any investment held in that capacity to be registered and held in the name of a nominee of the bank or title insurance company. The bank or title insurance company will be liable for the acts of any nominee with respect to any investment so registered.

The records of the bank or title insurance company must at all times show the ownership of the investment, and the investment must be in the possession and control of the bank or title insurance company and be kept separate from the assets of the bank or title insurance company (except that a state or national bank or title insurance company may deposit stock or other securities so held in a clearing corporation).

Settling a Trust after Death

On death of the settlor (the person who created the trust), a living trust must be "settled." Settling a living trust means administering and managing the trust according to the terms of the document. The person responsible for settling a trust is either the surviving trustee or the successor trustee. This chapter examines some of the issues attendant to settling a living trust.

Assets and Debts

After a settlor dies, the surviving or successor trustee must familiarize herself with the assets of the settlor, and determine whether all the assets have been placed in the trust. If an asset was not placed in trust, probate administration of that asset may be required.

Any asset held as community property with right of survivorship, or as joint tenants with the right of survivorship, automatically passes to the surviving owner. Any asset that has a "pay on death" beneficiary or a "transfer on death" beneficiary will be paid directly to the named beneficiary, regardless of any contrary language or instructions contained in the trust. If the trust is named as the beneficiary, the asset will be paid over to the trustee, and the terms of the trust will control the distribution of that asset.

After the settlor's death, the trustee should quickly move to determine whether the settlor was owed money. If so, the trustee should proceed to collect the debt. If the settlor owed money at the time of his death, the trustee generally should pay the settlor's debts as they become due. This is particularly true if the debt is secured by an asset of the trust, so as to not risk losing the asset through foreclosure or other means.

Estate Valuation

In settling a trust, the trustee must value the estate assets. Determining the value of the assets is important for a number of reasons. If the trust is an A-B trust, proper valuation will facilitate proper apportionment of the assets between the A (survivor's) Trust and B (decedent's) Trust. Proper valuation of assets will also allow the trustee to determine if estate taxes are due, and to calculate the amount of the tax obligation.

Under current law, assets receive a stepped-up basis on the settlor's death. This means that the value of the asset is the market value as of the date of death, and not what the settlor paid for the asset. The stepped-up basis generally benefits the beneficiary of the asset, who receives it at the higher valuation.

Tax Identification

In Arizona, an A-B Trust is created by a husband and wife. On the death of the first spouse, the trustee (generally the surviving spouse) must file IRS Form SS-4 to obtain a tax identification number for the B Trust. A separate tax identification number is needed for any trust that is created upon, or continues after, the death of the settlor.

It is a good idea to open a separate bank account for the B Trust (upon the death of the first spouse) and for the A Trust (on the death of the surviving spouse) in order to accurately document transactions in each trust. Each account will have a separate tax identification number.

Funding the Trusts

The trustee must determine which assets are to be kept in trust and which assets are to be distributed to the beneficiaries. Any specific bequests, whether for money or for a specified asset, should be distributed to the named beneficiary. The trustee should allocate the remaining assets to any new trusts (such as the A Trust and B Trust) created upon the death of the settlor. The trustee would be well advised to engage the help of a professional, such as an accountant, attorney, or financial advisor, in allocating the assets, because of the legal and tax implications involved.

Tax Returns

The trustee may be required to file tax returns as part of the settlement process. If income is generated from any of the assets of decedent held in trust, the trustee should file IRS Form 1041,

U.S. Income Tax Return for Estates and Trusts. On this income tax return, the trustee will report the income generated in the B Trust. Any income paid to a beneficiary (or the surviving spouse) is properly reported on the recipient's individual tax return, IRS Form 1040.

In some cases, it is necessary to file an estate tax return, IRS Form 706. An estate tax return is necessary if a person's estate exceeds the federal estate tax exemption. (Please refer to appendix A for information regarding the estate tax exemption amounts.) In the case of a married couple, no estate taxes are due upon the death of the first spouse, regardless of the amount of the estate. On the death of the surviving spouse, an estate tax return must be filed if the estate exceeds the estate tax exemption. In the case of an A-B-C Trust, commonly referred to as a QTIP Trust, an estate tax return must be filed to make a QTIP election for the C Trust. The trustee is advised to consult an accountant or qualified tax advisor to determine if a tax return is required.

PART TWO

Probate

Probate: An Overview

The term "probate" refers to the legal procedure for the administration of a deceased person's estate. In many cases, probate is a quick and efficient way to transfer the assets of a person who has died (the "decedent") to his heirs. (In other cases, the transfer of assets is best accomplished by the use of a trust or nonprobate transfers, which are discussed in other chapters of this book.) About ten thousand probate cases are filed each year in the state of Arizona.

The basic philosophy of the Arizona probate code is to minimize court involvement. It allows for the "informal" administration of most estates. This means that, in most cases, the entire probate procedure can be accomplished *without* court supervision or involvement. If an informal proceeding is not available or desired, the probate code provides for a "formal" proceeding. In a formal proceeding, the court is directly involved in the probate procedure.

Because informal probate proceedings are utilized in most cases, this chapter is devoted to the informal probate process in Arizona.

Opening the Estate

The first step in the administration of an estate is to have a person appointed to handle estate affairs. This person is known as the "personal representative" (formerly, this person was called the "executor"). To get a personal representative appointed, a person interested in the estate may file an application with the probate registrar (the registrar is a person authorized by law to make certain probate decisions, yet she is not a judge). An application for informal probate cannot be filed sooner than five days, nor later than two years, after the decedent's death.

If there is a will, an estate will normally be opened by an application for both informal probate of the will *and* appointment of a personal representative. A person nominated in a will has priority for appointment as personal representative. If there is no will, the probate application will merely request the appointment of a particular person to be the personal representative.

The following persons have priority (in the order listed) for appointment as personal representative: (1) the person nominated in a will, (2) the surviving spouse who is also a beneficiary under the will, (3) other will beneficiaries, (4) the surviving spouse, (5) other heirs, (6) forty-five days after the decedent's death, any creditor, and (7) the public fiduciary. Where several persons share priority, they must agree on which of them will be appointed as personal representative. If they are unable to agree, the court will appoint one or more of them in a formal proceeding.

Notice of Appointment

If a will is informally admitted to probate, the personal representative must give the heirs and each devisee (a devisee is a person designated in a will to receive estate assets) a written statement that the will has been admitted to probate by the court and that an heir has four months to contest the probate. A copy of the will must be sent with the statement.

The personal representative must also send a statement to the heirs and devisees informing them of the appointment, the personal representative's name and address, whether or not a bond has been filed, and a description of the court where official papers regarding the estate are on file. This statement may be combined with the statement described in the preceding paragraph. The statement must be given within ten days after the appointment of the personal representative.

Personal Representative's Duties

A personal representative is a fiduciary. This means that she has a duty of loyalty to the beneficiaries and creditors of the estate. The personal representative must be cautious and prudent in dealing with estate assets. The assets must never be used for the personal representative's benefit or mixed with other assets. A personal representative is prohibited by law from participating in any transaction that involves a conflict of interest.

The personal representative's first duty is to protect the estate property. This means that the personal representative must immediately find, identify, and take possession of the estate assets. If there is reason to believe that someone is concealing estate assets, the personal representative may file a lawsuit against the person who is hiding the assets. In that suit, the personal representative may examine the person regarding any property or papers relating to the decedent's estate.

The personal representative is required to prepare an inventory of the estate assets within ninety days after her appointment. The inventory must list all of the probate assets and their values as of the date of death. Once the inventory is prepared, the personal representative may file it with the court and mail a copy of it to the heirs and devisees or may simply mail a copy of it to the heirs and devisees. If the family does not want the information in the inventory to be made part of the public record, the personal representative should not file it with the court.

Family Allowances

The personal representative has the power to set allowances for the maintenance of the family during the probate process. These statutory allowances, as they are called, include a homestead allowance, exempt property allowance, and family allowance. The surviving spouse and dependent children are generally eligible to receive these allowances, in the amounts set by statute.

Claims of Creditors

The personal representative must publish notice to creditors once a week for three successive weeks in a newspaper of general circulation in the county of appointment. The notice will announce the appointment of the personal representative and tell creditors of the estate that they must present their claims to the personal representative, at the address specified in the notice, within four months from the date of first publication. If a claim is not presented within the four-month creditors' claim period, generally it will not be paid. A notice must also be mailed by the personal representative to all persons whom she knows are creditors or those who can be reasonably ascertained.

If a claim is disputed, the personal representative may disallow it or negotiate a compromise with the person making it. The personal representative has a duty to investigate each claim and decide whether to allow it or disallow it. To disallow a claim, the personal representative must, within sixty days after the time for presentation has expired, file a notice of disallowance and notify the claimant accordingly. Failure by the personal representative to disallow the claim has the effect of allowing it.

The personal representative must pay all valid debts and expenses (including taxes) owed by the estate. If there are not enough assets to pay all of the charges against the estate, the personal representative must determine which debts and expenses should be paid according to law. The personal representative may be personally liable to the beneficiaries or to creditors with unpaid claims if she pays a debt or expense that should not be paid.

Distribution of Assets

After payment of all debts and expenses, the personal representative must distribute the remaining assets as directed in the will. If there is no will, the assets must be distributed to the heirs as provided by law. The personal representative owes a duty of impartiality to all heirs and devisees under a will. This means that they must all be treated alike. Nonetheless, the personal representative, in some cases, may distribute the assets in cash or in kind, or partially in cash and partially in kind. For distributions in kind, the property must be valued at fair market value at the time of distribution. The personal representative may be personally liable if she makes an improper distribution of estate assets.

Personal Representative's Compensation

The personal representative is entitled to reasonable compensation for her services. Arizona law does not designate percentage fees for the personal representative's work or state how much she should be paid for her services. The personal representative should keep detailed records of all time expended by her on estate matters and receipts to prove out-of-pocket expenses. In determining whether a fee is reasonable, several factors will be considered, including the time required, the fee normally charged for similar services, the nature and value of estate assets, and the results obtained for the estate.

The personal representative must prepare a final account at the end of the administration process. The account must contain a full disclosure of the handling of the estate, including income received, expenses paid, and gains or losses on the sale of estate assets. The account must be sent to all persons who are affected by it.

The court supervises neither informal probates nor the conduct of the personal representatives who handle them. However, if any person who has an interest in the estate believes that the estate has not been properly handled or that the fees charged by the attorney or personal representative are not reasonable under the circumstances, he or she may request that the court review the personal representative's accounting.

Closing the Estate

After distribution of the estate has been completed, the estate must be closed. To close an estate informally, the personal representative will file a verified statement (known as a "closing statement") affirming that she has (1) published notice to creditors, (2) fully administered the estate (including settlement of claims, expenses, and taxes, and distribution of the assets), (3) sent a copy to all distributees and to creditors with unpaid claims, and (4) furnished an account to all interested parties. The court will usually expect the estate to be completely administered and closed by no later than one year after the appointment of the personal representative.

The personal representative cannot be sued for breach of duties after six months from the filing of the closing statement, except for fraud, misrepresentation, or inadequate disclosure. The appointment of the personal representative terminates one year after the closing statement is filed, unless proceedings are pending.

Rules for Determining Heirs

The Arizona Probate Code provides rules for determining heirs. These rules apply in cases where the deceased person (the "decedent") fails to leave a will or where not all of the decedent's assets are disposed of by the will (or by one or more nonprobate transfers). In those cases, the Code determines the decedent's heirs and the shares to which those heirs are entitled.

The rules are:

» If the decedent was survived by a spouse but no issue (children, grandchildren, or other descendants), then all assets to spouse.

» If the decedent was survived by a spouse and issue, all of whom are also issue of the surviving spouse, then all assets to spouse.

» If the decedent was survived by a spouse and issue, one or more of whom are not issue of the surviving spouse, then one-half of the decedent's separate property to spouse, and the decedent's half of community property and one-half of the decedent's separate property to issue.

» If the decedent was survived by issue but no spouse, then all assets to issue (by right of representation).*

» If the decedent was not survived by a spouse or issue, then all assets to surviving parents equally.

» If the decedent was not survived by a spouse, issue, or parent, then all assets to brothers and sisters equally (the issue of a deceased sibling, i.e., nephews and nieces, take by representation).

» If the decedent was not survived by a spouse, issue, parent, sibling, or issue of a sibling, then one-half of assets to paternal grand-parents equally (or their issue if both are deceased) and one-half of assets to maternal grandparents equally (or their issue if both deceased).

» If the decedent was not survived by a grand-parent or issue on one side of the family,

---

* "By representation" means that an heir takes assets by representation of a deceased parent. For example, three children of a deceased parent would each take by representation one-third of their parent's share.

then all assets to grandparents or their issue on the other side.

» If the decedent was not survived by issue of parents or grandparents, then all assets to state of Arizona.

Some other rules:

» The terms of a valid will supersede the above rules (i.e., the terms of a will replace any rule).

» A person who does not survive the decedent by 120 hours is deemed not to have survived the decedent.

» Relatives of the half blood inherit the same share as if they were of the whole blood.

» A child in gestation is treated as living at that time if the child lives at least 120 hours after its birth.

» A person is the child of his natural parents, regardless of their marital status.

» An adopted person is the child of his adopting parents.

Protection against Disinheritance

Disinheritance is the omission of a spouse or children from a will. This chapter examines the protections against disinheritance provided under Arizona law.

The principal protection of a surviving spouse against disinheritance is her share in the community property. Each spouse has the power to dispose of only his or her half of the community property, as well as his or her separate property. Arizona law gives either spouse power separately to dispose of community property, except that both must join in disposition of most interests in real property.

Omitted Spouse

If a person executes a will and later marries, Arizona law gives the surviving spouse an intestate share[*] unless: (1) the will showed that the

---

[*] Intestate share means a share of an estate determined by law, as opposed to a share specified under a person's will.

spouse's omission was intentional, (2) the will states that it is to be effective notwithstanding any subsequent marriage, or (3) the testator (the person who executes a will) made a transfer of property outside the will which can be shown to have been intended as a substitute for provision by will. However, this rule does not apply to any property bequeathed to the testator's child or children who are born prior to the testator's marriage to the surviving spouse. Because it is common for such an individual to have a will leaving everything to the children from a prior marriage, it is possible that an omitted spouse will also be a disinherited spouse.

Omitted Children

Children born or adopted after execution of a will may be unintentionally omitted from the will, in which case they are entitled to an intestate share. Children receive no intestate share if there is a surviving spouse and the children of the decedent are also the children of the surviving spouse. This means the omitted children will benefit only when: (1) there is no surviving spouse, or (2) there is a spouse but the children of the testator are by a prior marriage.

The omission of a child is treated as unintentional except in the following situations: (1) when the testator's will shows intent to exclude an after-born child, (2) where the will, executed when the testator has one or more children, leaves substantially all his estate to his wife, who is the mother of the after-born child, and (3) where the testator provides for the after-born child by a transfer outside the will, which is intended to be in lieu of a share in the estate.

Allowances and Exempt Property

An allowance is a sum of money payable to a deceased person's (the "decedent's") spouse and children, before payment of any of the decedent's debts. Allowances operate as a protection against disinheritance by the testator (the person who executes a will) since these are rights conferred by statute. They also protect the family against creditors because the allowances take precedence over all creditors' claims except the expenses of administration.

Under Arizona law, if the decedent was domiciled in Arizona, the surviving spouse can claim the following: (1) an allowance in lieu of homestead in the amount of $18,000, (2) an exempt property allowance in the amount of $7,000, and (3) a reasonable allowance for maintenance during the period of administration, known as a family allowance.

If there is no surviving spouse, the decedent's children who are either minors or dependents of the decedent are entitled to the homestead allowance and the family allowance; and the decedent's children, whether or not they are minors or dependents, are entitled to the exempt property allowance. If no spouse or child survived the decedent, then there is no right under these allowances.

The allowances and exempt property are chargeable against any provision for the spouse or children in the will unless otherwise provided by the will. Also, they are chargeable against any intestate share* of the spouse or children.

Allowance in Lieu of Homestead

The allowance in lieu of homestead is a dollar amount, $18,000. Unlike the lifetime homestead exemption, the probate allowance in lieu of homestead is more limited in amount and is not tied to the ownership of a home. During lifetime, any person over eighteen residing in Arizona may hold as a homestead a residence exempt from attachment by creditors not exceeding $150,000 in value. That right ceases at death. Although only one homestead exemption may be claimed by a married couple, upon the death of a spouse, the surviving spouse may claim both the allowance in lieu of homestead and the homestead exemption.

A surviving spouse may claim the allowance in lieu of homestead where: (1) the decedent and his spouse owned no house but lived in a rented apartment, (2) the decedent owned a house, or

---

* Intestate share means a share of an estate determined by law, as opposed to a share specified under a person's will.

(3) the decedent and spouse owned a home in joint tenancy with right of survivorship.

Exempt Property

In addition to the allowance in lieu of homestead, the spouse or children of a decedent can claim $7,000 in household furniture, automobiles, furnishings, appliances, and personal effects. If the estate does not have $7,000 in the types of property enumerated above, then other property may be selected to make up the deficiency. The law provides, however, that specifically devised property cannot be used for the allowances and exempt property if there is other property in sufficient amount. For example, if the decedent specifically willed his car and some of his personal effects to a brother, the spouse or children could not claim the car unless all other property in the estate was insufficient to satisfy their rights.

Family Allowance

The surviving spouse and dependent children are entitled to a living allowance during administration. This allowance is flexible, and much is left to the determination of the personal representative (the person who administers the will following the testator's death) and the court. The law provides for a "reasonable allowance," and what is reasonable depends on many factors. Some factors include the previous standard of living and the nature of other resources available to the family to meet current living expenses until the estate can be administered and assets distributed. While the death of the principal income producer may necessitate some change in the standard of living, there must also be a period of adjustment. If the surviving spouse has a substantial income, this may be taken into account.

The allowance may be paid in a lump sum or in periodic installments. The law gives the personal representative discretionary power to set an allowance not exceeding $12,000 in a lump sum or $1,000 a month for one year. If a greater allowance is needed, a court order must be sought. If someone, like a creditor, thinks the amount set by the representative is unreasonable, that person may petition the court to reduce the amount.

Normally the allowance is payable to the surviving spouse for the benefit of the spouse and the dependent children. If a dependent child is not living with the spouse, however, part of the allowance can be paid to the spouse and part to the dependent child (or a guardian or other person having care and custody) as the child's needs appear.

Small Estate Affidavits

It is possible to avoid probate entirely in small estates by using affidavits to collect the property and assets of the deceased person (the "decedent"). This chapter explains how to use small estate affidavits to avoid probate.

Hypothetical Case

Let us use a hypothetical case to explore the process. Our hypothetical case involves a decedent who was married shortly before his untimely death. The decedent owned a modest home, a car, a few shares of stock in his employer's company, and a bank account.

Because our decedent was recently married, he had not yet updated his estate plan to allow his estate to pass outside of probate to his wife by survivorship in joint tenancy and community property or by beneficiary designations on his accounts. All of his property was titled solely in his name at the time of his death. He did not leave a will. (The decedent in this hypothetical case is not unlike many people who put off estate planning until it is too late.)

Affidavit to Collect Wages

Fortunately, probate may still be avoided in this case. Wages or salary due the decedent may be collected by his wife by furnishing to his employer an affidavit that meets a few simple requirements. The affidavit must state that the affiant (the person making the affidavit) is the surviving spouse of the decedent or is authorized to act on behalf of the spouse and that no application for the appointment of a personal representative is pending or has been granted (if one was granted, the personal representative must have been discharged, or more than one year must have passed since the filing of a closing statement).

This affidavit may be used any time after the death of the decedent. There is no waiting period. However, payment is limited to $5,000 by the use of this affidavit (not a problem in our hypothetical case).

Affidavit to Collect Personal Property

A separate affidavit must be used to collect the decedent's personal property, such as the money in his bank account, his company stock, and his car. The requirements for this affidavit are different from those for the affidavit to collect wages discussed in the preceding section, but they are no more difficult. The decedent's spouse must wait 30 days after the decedent's death to use this affidavit.

The affidavit must contain the following statements:

» Thirty days have elapsed since the death of the decedent.

» Either: (a) an application for the appointment of a personal representative is not pending and a personal representative has not been appointed and the value of all personal property in the decedent's estate does not exceed $50,000 (as valued as of the date of death) or (b) the personal representative has been discharged or more than one year has passed since the filing of a closing statement, and the value of all property in the decedent's estate does not exceed $50,000 (as valued as of the date of the affidavit).

» The person presenting the affidavit (or on whose behalf the affidavit is presented) is entitled to the property.

Note that all of the decedent's property, wherever located, must be included in the valuation determination, minus liens and encumbrances. When the personal property affidavit is presented by the decedent's wife to the bank, the bank will close the decedent's account and issue a cashier's check to the widow.

Similarly, when the affidavit is presented to the company's stock transfer agent, together with the stock certificate, the stock will be reissued in the widow's name. (It may be more convenient to have a stockbroker handle the stock transfer for a small fee.)

The motor vehicle division will transfer title of the decedent's vehicle to the widow upon presentation of the affidavit and on payment of the necessary fees.

Because the value of the decedent's personal property in our hypothetical case does not exceed $50,000, the decedent's spouse is able to collect all of it by affidavit.

Affidavit to Collect Real Estate

The sole remaining asset in our hypothetical case is the decedent's house. The assessment for the year in which the decedent died showed the full cash value of the property to be $150,000. The decedent owed $125,000 to the mortgage company at the time of his death.

The decedent's spouse can again use an affidavit to acquire title to the property, but she must wait six months to do so. Once the six-month waiting period is over, the decedent's spouse may file in the superior court in the county in which the decedent was domiciled at the time of his death an affidavit describing the real property and the interest of the decedent in the property. The affidavit must contain specific statements required by the statute and must have certain documents attached to it. Any false statement in the affidavit may subject the person to penalties for perjury. The real property affidavit does have certain limitations: (1) the value of the property, less all liens and encumbrances, cannot exceed $50,000, (2) the affidavit cannot be used if an application for the appointment of a personal representative is pending or if one has been appointed, (3) the affidavit cannot be filed sooner than six months after the decedent's death, (4) the decedent's funeral expenses and debts must have been be paid, and (5) no estate tax can be due on the decedent's estate.

The requirements for the affidavit are set forth more specifically in ARS Section 14-3971(E), the text of which can be downloaded from the Arizona State Legislature's website, www.azleg. state.az.us, or obtained from most public libraries in Arizona.

On receipt of the properly completed affidavit (and any necessary attachments), the probate registrar will issue a certified copy of the affidavit to the filer. The certified copy must then be recorded in the office of the recorder in the county where the real property is located.

As the above hypothetical case illustrates, affidavits can be used in Arizona to collect wages and salaries up to $5,000, to collect personal property up to $50,000, and to transfer title to real property having a net value of not more than $50,000. When affidavits are used in lieu of probate, the cost savings can be considerable.

Nonprobate Transfers of Bank Accounts

Checking accounts, savings accounts, certificates of deposit, and credit union share accounts all may be transferred outside of probate. This chapter shows how this can be done.

Pay on Death Designation

A "pay on death" designation* means the designation of (1) a beneficiary in an account payable to one party during the party's lifetime and, on the party's death, to one or more beneficiaries or (2) a beneficiary in an account in the name of one or more parties as trustee for one or more beneficiaries. The second designation is sometimes referred to as "in trust for," but by law it is a pay on death designation.

On the death of the sole party or the last survivor of two or more parties in an account with a pay on death designation, the sums on

* Note: Any designation discussed in this chapter must be established with the financial institution at which the account is located.

deposit belong to the surviving beneficiary or beneficiaries. If two or more beneficiaries survive, the money belongs to them in equal shares.

Right of Survivorship

On the death of a party, the sums on deposit in a multiple party account belong to the surviving party or parties. If two or more parties survive and one is the surviving spouse of the deceased party (the "decedent"), the amount to which the decedent, immediately before death, was entitled belongs to the surviving spouse. If two or more parties survive and none is the surviving spouse, the decedent's share belongs to the surviving parties in equal shares. The right of survivorship continues between the surviving parties.

Estate Planning Considerations

The type of account is established by the party or parties owning it. An account may be changed by written notice given to the financial institution to change the account or to stop or vary payment under the terms of the account. As shown above, probate is not necessary to transfer ownership of sums on deposit in an account with a pay on death designation or one with the right of survivorship. Because avoiding probate is desirable, consideration should be given to employing these types of accounts for estate planning purposes.

Beneficiary Deeds to Avoid Probate

A deed is a legal document that transfers an interest in real estate to another person. Anyone who owns a house acquired title to it by a deed. In this chapter, we will see how real property can be transferred outside of probate by using a beneficiary deed.

A beneficiary deed conveys an interest in real property to another person, called the beneficiary, on the *death* of the property owner. The transfer is subject to all liens and encumbrances on the property at the time of the owner's death. A beneficiary deed can be used by an owner of real property to transfer that property on her death *outside of probate*. A beneficiary deed may designate multiple beneficiaries and state how those beneficiaries will take title to the property.

If the property is owned by more than one person, all of the owners should sign the beneficiary deed. If the property is owned as joint tenants with the right of survivorship or as community property with the right of survivorship, and all of the owners execute the beneficiary deed, the deed is effective on the death of the last surviving owner. (Special rules apply if less than all of the owners sign the beneficiary deed.)

A beneficiary deed is valid only if it is executed and recorded as provided by law in the office of the county recorder in the county in which the property is located, before the death of the owner or the last surviving owner.

The chief characteristic of a beneficiary deed is that the transfer of the owner's interest in the property is not effective until the owner's death. Thus, the beneficiary does not acquire any interest in the property during the owner's lifetime.

A beneficiary deed may be revoked at any time by the owner or owners who executed it. To be effective, the revocation must be executed and recorded in the county recorder's office before the death of the owner or the last surviving owner, if there are survivorship rights. A beneficiary deed cannot be revoked by the provisions of a will.

Because a beneficiary deed may be used to avoid probate, it should be considered as part of any comprehensive estate plan.

PART THREE

Powers of Attorney and Medical Directives

Durable Powers of Attorney

A durable power of attorney is an important component of any comprehensive estate plan. Simply stated, a durable power of attorney is a document by which one person appoints another person to make financial decisions for him if he is subsequently disabled or incapacitated. Properly executed, it can save both time and money in managing the financial affairs of a person who becomes disabled or incapacitated.

In a durable power of attorney, one person (the "principal") designates another person as his agent. Both the principal and agent must be eighteen years of age or older. The document must contain words showing the principal's intent that the authority granted in the durable power of attorney may be exercised if the principal is subsequently disabled or incapacitated, regardless of how much time has elapsed (unless the document states a termination date).

By executing a written power of attorney, a principal may designate an agent to make financial decisions on the principal's behalf. The power of attorney must contain language that clearly identifies the agent and shows that the principal intends to create a power of attorney. It must be signed by the principal (or, in rare cases, by someone else for the principal), and must be properly witnessed and notarized. The witness cannot be the agent, the agent's spouse, the agent's child, or the notary public. (The execution requirements are set forth in ARS Section 14-5501, the text of which is available on the Arizona State Legislature's website, www.azleg. state.az.us.)

A person may nominate in a durable power of attorney a conservator or guardian for consideration by the court if protective proceedings for him or his estate are commenced. (Guardianship and conservatorship proceedings are discussed in part four.)

Any act carried out by an agent pursuant to a durable power of attorney while the principal is disabled or incapacitated binds the principal as if he were not incapacitated or disabled.

The law requires an agent to use the principal's money, property, or other assets only in the principal's best interest. Thus, the agent cannot use the principal's money, property, or other assets for her own benefit. An agent who violates this law is subject to criminal prosecution and civil penalties.

The only exception to the above "best interest" rule is where the principal specifically authorizes the agent to use his money, property, or other assets in a way that is not in his best interest or is for the agent's best interest. However, this authority must be in writing, and special execution requirements apply.

Some Other Rules

»   A power of attorney executed in another state is valid in Arizona if it was validly executed in the state in which it was created.

»   If the agent acted with intimidation or deception in obtaining the power of attorney, she is subject to criminal prosecution and civil penalties.

»   A power of attorney is invalid if it was executed by an adult who was incapable of understanding, in a reasonable manner, the nature and effect of his actions.

»   A power of attorney may be revoked by the principal.

»   A power of attorney may contain a termination date.

»   The death of the principal terminates the authority granted to the agent by the document (when the agent learns of the principal's death).

»   A durable power of attorney does not establish authority for an agent to make health care decisions for her principal. (This topic is discussed in the chapter on health care directives.)

Legal Tip:

As with other estate planning documents, it is important that the power of attorney be properly drafted and executed. For this reason, an attorney should be consulted to handle the matter. (For the price, it is fairly cheap insurance to protect against drafting and execution errors.)

Delegation of Parental Powers

In Arizona, a parent of a minor (under age eighteen) may delegate to another person any powers she may have regarding the care, custody, or property of the minor child, except the power to consent to marriage or adoption of the minor.

A parent desiring to delegate her parental powers pursuant to this law must execute a power of attorney. (For the legal requirements of this document, please refer to the preceding chapter on durable powers of attorney.) A parent cannot delegate her parental powers by a power of attorney for longer than six months, but there is no limitation on the number of powers of attorney that she may execute. The six-month period may thus be extended by the execution of successive six-month powers of attorney.

Any parent leaving her child in the care of another for an extended period of time would do well to consider delegating some or all of her parental powers to the child's temporary caregiver. By so doing, a parent may be able to avoid the consequences of Murphy's Law ("If anything can go wrong, it will").

Health Care Directives

A health care directive is, as the name implies, a document prepared to deal with a person's future health care decisions. In Arizona, there are three types of health care directives: (1) a health care power of attorney, (2) a prehospital medical care directive, and (3) a mental health care power of attorney. A living will, which may be either attached to a health care power of attorney or executed separately, is discussed in the next chapter.

Why a chapter on health care directives? Because health care directives constitute an important part of any comprehensive estate plan. Every person implementing an estate plan in Arizona should give serious consideration to executing one or more health care directives.

Each type of directive is discussed below.

1. Health Care Power of Attorney

A health care power of attorney is a written designation of an agent to make health care decisions. It is a durable power of attorney, which means that it survives the person's subsequent disability or incompetency. (For a durable health care power of attorney form, see appendix B.)

A person who is eighteen years of age or older (the "principal") may designate another adult (the "agent") to make health care decisions on that person's behalf. The health care power of attorney must meet certain legal requirements, including that it be dated, signed, and notarized or witnessed by at least one adult. The principal must appear to be of sound mind and free from duress at the time the health care power of attorney is signed.

An agent designated in a health care power of attorney has full power to give or refuse consent to all medical, surgical, hospital, and related health care. The power of attorney is only effective on the inability of the principal to make or communicate health care decisions. If the principal has also executed a living will, the agent will be directed to implement those choices that the principal initialed in the living will.

An amendment to the power of attorney, unless made only to indicate an agent's change of address or phone number, must meet all of the legal requirements applicable to executing the original document. A health care power of attorney, once made, continues in effect until those who may rely on it have notice of its revocation.

2. *Prehospital Medical Care Directive*

A prehospital medical care directive (DNR) is a document that, in the event of cardiac or respiratory arrest by the patient, directs the with-holding of cardiopulmonary resuscitation by emergency medical system and hospital emergency department personnel. (For a prehospital medical care directive form, see appendix C.) Withholding of cardiopulmonary resuscitation pursuant to a prehospital medical care directive does not, however, include the withholding of other medical interventions, such as intravenous fluids, oxygen, or other therapies deemed necessary to provide comfort care or to alleviate pain.

A prehospital medical care directive must be printed on an orange background and may be in either letter or wallet size. A person who has a valid prehospital medical care directive may wear an identifying bracelet on either his wrist or his ankle. The bracelet must be similar to identification bracelets worn in hospitals, be on an orange background, and state certain information in bold type.

3. *Mental Health Care Power of Attorney*

An adult, known as the principal, may designate another adult or adults to act as agent and to make mental health care decisions on the principal's behalf. The principal may also designate an alternate adult or adults to act as agent if the original designated agent or agents are unwilling or unable to act. (For a durable mental health care power of attorney form, see appendix D.)

The agent may make decisions about the mental health treatment on behalf of the principal if the principal is found incapable. If an adult does not have a mental health care power of attorney, an agent with a health care power of attorney (discussed in section one above) may make decisions about mental health treatment on behalf of the principal if the principal is found incapable. However, an agent may not consent to admit the principal to a level one behavioral health facility unless the authority is expressly stated in the power of attorney.

The decisions about mental health treatment on behalf of the principal must be consistent with any wishes the principal has expressed in the mental health care directive, mental health care power of attorney, health care power of attorney, or other advance directive.

Note about Legal Requirements for Directives

Due to space limitations, not all of the legal requirements for the health care directives discussed in this chapter have been included. For each type of directive, there are a host of specific requirements that must be followed. The requirements are set forth in sections 36-3201 through 36-3287 of the Arizona Revised Statutes. For those interested, the text of those statutes may be obtained from the Arizona State Legislature's website, www.azleg.state.az.us.

Consistent with the author's advice concerning the drafting and execution of other estate planning documents discussed in this book, the author recommends that an attorney be retained to draft and oversee the execution of all health care directives. By using an attorney, legal compliance will be assured.

Living Wills

A living will is a written statement composed by a person and intended to guide or control the health care treatment decisions that can be made on her behalf. (For a living will form, see appendix F.) Contrary to what may be suggested by the name, a living will is not legally related to a *will* or to a *living trust* (although all three documents may be written as part of a comprehensive estate plan).

A person may write and use a living will without writing a health care power of attorney[*] or may attach a living will to her health care power of attorney. (If the living will is not part of a health care power of attorney, the person must verify it in the same manner as required for a health care power of attorney.) If a person has a health care power of attorney, the agent must make health care decisions that are consistent with the person's known desires and that are

---

[*] For a discussion on health care powers of attorney, please see the preceding chapter on health care directives.

medically reasonable and appropriate. A person can, but is not required to, state her desires in a living will.

In a typical living will, the person writing it will answer the following basic questions relating to her health care:

» If you have a terminal condition, do you *not* want your life to be prolonged, and do you *not* want life-sustaining treatment (beyond comfort care) that would serve only to artificially delay the moment of your death?

» If you are in a terminal condition or an irreversible coma or a persistent vegetative state which your doctors reasonably feel to be irreversible or incurable, do you want the medical treatment necessary to provide care that would keep you comfortable but *not* cardiopulmonary resuscitation, artificially administered food and fluids, and/or to be taken to a hospital if at all avoidable?

» (For women only) If you are known to be pregnant, do you want life-sustaining treatment used if it is possible that the embryo/fetus will develop to the point of live birth with the continued application of life-sustaining treatment?

» Do you want the use of all medical care necessary to treat your condition until your doctors reasonably conclude that your condition is terminal or is irreversible and incurable or you are in a persistent vegetative state?

» Do you want your life to be prolonged to the greatest extent possible?

A person writing a living will is free to make other or additional statements of desires and attach additional special provisions or limitations to the document. In that a living will is intended to guide or control the health care treatment decisions that can be made on that person's behalf, it should be as specific and personal as possible.

Organ Donation

Donating organs saves lives. Approximately 300 new organ transplant candidates are added to a waiting list each month, and the number of people waiting for a transplant is increasing. This chapter is for people who wish to donate all or part of their body by making an anatomical gift.

In Arizona, every person is eligible to be an organ donor; there are no age or physical limitations. Even if a donor has a preexisting medical condition, organ transplant teams may find a suitable use for the person's organs.

For a person interested in donating organs, it is vitally important that his wish to be an organ donor be *known* at the time of death. A person can make known his desire to be an organ donor in a number of ways, including by executing a health care power of attorney, completing a donor card, registering with the Donor Network of Arizona, and informing his family members.

Health Care Power of Attorney

A health care power of attorney is a written designation of an agent to make health care decisions. It is a durable power of attorney, which means that it survives the person's subsequent disability or incompetency.

By executing a health care power of attorney, a person formally states his specific desires about organ donation. In this document, a person can: (a) choose to donate any needed organs or parts or only specified parts or organs; (b) choose to donate organs for any legally authorized purpose (transplantation, therapy, medical and dental evaluation and research, and/or advancement of medical and dental science) or for transplant or therapeutic purposes only (the organs will go to a person in need for the purpose of healing); and (c) designate a specific individual or institution to receive his tissues or organs or authorize his representative to make that decision. In lieu of the foregoing, a person can declare, in a health care power of attorney, that he does *not* want to make an organ or tissue donation and he does *not* want a donation authorized on his behalf by his representative or his family. (For a durable health care power of attorney form, see appendix B.)

Donor Card

A uniform donor card (appendix G) may also evidence a person's desire to become an organ donor. On this card, the donor states his wish to donate his organs and tissues (either any needed organs and tissues or specified organs and tissues). The donor must sign and date the card in the presence of two witnesses, and he should then keep the card in his wallet or another readily accessible place.

Donor Network of Arizona

The Donor Network of Arizona is a registry for persons who desire to become organ donors. (For more information, you may visit their website: www.dnaz.org.) Registration on the donor network is the best way for a person to make known his desire to become an organ donor.

The Donor Network of Arizona accesses a national computer system to determine where donated organs will go. The network coordinator receives a list of patients who are waiting for, and need, the organs donated. A patient's priority for organs depends on a number of factors, including medical urgency, the time on the waiting list, tissue match, geography, and—for hearts, livers, and lungs—blood type and body size.

It should be noted that a person not registered with the Donor Network of Arizona can still become an organ donor if he has made known his desire to his family or health care agent. A family notification form (appendix G) can serve to notify family members of a person's intention to be an organ donor. The family or health care agent of a person who dies is almost always asked if the decedent wished to be an organ donor.

Donated Organs and Tissues

If a person elects to donate other than "any organ or body part," he will specify what organs or tissues he chooses to donate. A person may choose to donate any or all of the following organs: heart, kidneys, pancreas, lungs, liver, and intestines. In addition, he may choose to donate any or all of the following tissues: skin, cornea, bone marrow, heart valves, and connective tissue.

Organ donation does not disfigure the body and does not preclude an open casket at the funeral. The donor's family is not liable for costs of organ donation; all costs of organ donation are paid by the recipient of an organ (usually through insurance).

PART FOUR

Property and Gifts

Ways to Take Title to Real Estate in Arizona

When a person buys a house, rental property, or a vacation home, she takes title to the property. This chapter examines and compares the different ways to take title to real estate in Arizona.

» **Community Property.** To take title as community property, the title holders must have a valid marriage. Each spouse holds an undivided one-half interest in the estate. One spouse cannot partition the property by selling his or her interest. The signatures of both spouses are required to convey title or encumber the property. Each spouse can devise (through a will) one-half of the community property. Upon death, the estate of the decedent must be "cleared" through probate, affidavit, or adjudication (court action). Both halves of the community property are entitled to a stepped-up tax basis as of the date of death.

» **Joint Tenancy with Right of Survivorship.** The parties need not be married to take title as joint tenants, and there may be more than two joint tenants. Each joint tenant holds an equal and undivided interest in the estate. There is unity of interest. One joint tenant can partition the property by selling his or her joint interest. The signatures of all joint tenants are required to convey or encumber the whole. The estate passes to the surviving tenant or tenants outside of probate. No court action is required to clear title upon the death of a joint tenant. The deceased tenant's share is entitled to a stepped-up tax basis as of the date of death.

» **Community Property with Right of Survivorship.** This method of taking title combines the most favorable characteristics of the first two methods. Because title is taken as community property, the parties must be married. As with the first method (community property *without* the right of survivorship), each spouse holds an undivided one-half interest in the estate. One spouse cannot partition the property by selling his or her interest, and the signatures of both spouses are required to convey title or encumber the property. However unlike the first method, no court action is required to clear title upon the first death (this feature is common to joint tenancy with right of survivorship). Both halves of the community property are entitled to a stepped-up tax basis as of the date of death.

» **Tenancy in Common.** The parties need not be married to take title as tenants in common, and there may be more than two tenants in common. Each tenant in common holds an undivided fractional interest in the estate. The fractional interests can be disproportionate (e.g., 20 percent and 80 percent; 40 percent and 60 percent; 20 percent, 20 percent, and 60 percent; etc.). Each tenant's share can be conveyed, mortgaged or devised to a third party. The signatures of all of the tenants are required to convey or encumber the whole. Upon death, the tenant's proportionate share passes to his or her heirs. The estate of the decedent must be cleared through probate, affidavit, or adjudication. Each share has its own tax basis.

Arizona is a community property state. Property acquired by a husband and wife is presumed to be community property, unless legally specified differently.

Title may be held as "sole and separate." If a married person acquires title as sole and separate property, her spouse must execute a disclaimer deed to avoid the presumption of community property.

Parties may choose to hold title in the name of an entity. The entity holding title may be a corporation, limited liability company, partnership, or a trust.

Each method of taking title has certain legal and tax consequences. Accordingly, the reader is encouraged to obtain competent legal and tax advice before taking title to her next house, rental property, or vacation home.

Lifetime Gifts

Gifts of property may be made by a person during his lifetime or after his death. This chapter deals with lifetime gifts. Gifts made after death are discussed generally in the chapters on wills and trusts and nonprobate transfers.

Property is divided into two basic types: personal property and real property. "Personal property" is all property other than real property. "Real property" is synonymous with real estate and interests in real estate. The gift rules are different for each type of property.

Gifts of Personal Property

To make a valid lifetime gift of personal property, the gift must be in writing, duly acknowledged and recorded, or actual possession of the gift must be passed to and remain with the donee (the gift recipient) or someone claiming under her. The rules for making gifts to minors are set forth in the next chapter.

Gifts of Real Property

To make a valid lifetime gift of real property, the transfer must be evidenced by a properly executed deed or instrument of conveyance, and delivered by the party making the gift, or by his authorized agent. Every deed or conveyance of real property must be signed by the donor (the person making the gift) and properly notarized. The deed or instrument of conveyance should be recorded in the office of the county recorder where the property is located.

Gift Tax

A person who makes a gift of property during his lifetime may be subject to federal gift tax. Most gifts are not subject to the gift tax, however. There is usually no tax if the gift is made to a spouse. If a gift is made to someone else, the gift tax does not apply until the value of the gifts to that person is more than the annual exclusion for the year.

A separate annual exclusion applies to each person to whom a gift is made. The annual exclusion in 2008 is $12,000 per person. The annual exclusion may be increased in any year due to a cost-of-living adjustment. A person contemplating making a gift should consult his tax advisor or contact the Internal Revenue Service for the current amount of the annual exclusion.

Even if tax applies to a person's gifts, he will generally be able to eliminate or reduce the gift tax by using the so-called unified credit. (We are now getting into tax law, which is beyond the scope of this handbook. For those interested in this subject, the author suggests obtaining a copy of IRS Publication 950, Introduction to Estate and Gift Taxes. This publication may be obtained online from the IRS's website, www. irs.gov, or by requesting a copy by fax, 703-368-9694.)

Generally, a person will need to file a gift tax return only if a gift is made to someone other than that person's spouse *and* the value of the gift is more than the gift tax exclusion for that year. A person who receives a gift will not have to pay any gift tax because of it, nor will that person have to pay income tax on the value of the gift.

A person making a gift cannot deduct the value of the gift unless the gift is made to a qualified charity. In that case, the gift may be a deductible charitable contribution. Here, again, a qualified tax advisor should be consulted before the gift is made.

Gifts to Minors

Gifts to minors may be made pursuant to the Arizona Uniform Transfers to Minors Act. The act makes gift-giving to minors relatively easy and inexpensive. This chapter discusses the process of giving gifts to minors under the Act.

A gift to a minor may consist of stock, money, ownership of a life insurance policy or annuity contract, a right to future payments under a contract, an interest in real estate, or a certificate of title to a vehicle. The list is not inclusive in that an interest in virtually any property may be transferred to a minor under the Act.

The process to transfer property to a minor is fairly simple. The person making the gift appoints an adult over twenty-one years of age or a trust company as *custodian* for the minor. The custodian then takes control of the property until the minor attains the age of eighteen or twenty-one years (depending on the manner by which the gift was made) or until the minor dies. A gift may also be made pursuant to a person's will or trust or, under certain circumstances, by a person's personal representative or trustee.

The following language must generally

be used in connection with the transfer of any property to a custodian: "As custodian for _____ (name of minor) under the Arizona Uniform Transfer to Minors Act." The transfer requirements for different kinds of property are set forth in the statute, ARS Section 14-7659, which should be consulted prior to any property transfer. (A copy of the statute may be obtained at most public libraries or online from the Arizona State Legislature's website, www. azleg.state.az.us.)

Duties of Custodian

A custodian must take control of the minor's property, register or record title to it if appropriate, and collect, hold, manage, invest, and reinvest the property. In dealing with the property (which is referred to as the "custodial property"), a custodian must observe the standard of care that would be observed by a "prudent person" dealing with the property of another. If a custodian has a special skill or expertise, she must use it.

A custodian must keep the custodial property separate from all other property, sufficient to identify it clearly as custodial property of the minor. The custodian must also keep records of all transactions with respect to the custodial property. The records must be made available to a parent of the minor or to the minor if she is at least fourteen years of age.

Use of Custodial Property; Custodian's

Expenses

A custodian may deliver or pay to the minor, or expend for the minor's benefit, as much of the custodial property as the custodian considers advisable for the minor's use and benefit.

A custodian is entitled to reimbursement from the custodial property for reasonable expenses incurred in the performance of her duties.

Successor Custodian

A person who is nominated to be a custodian may decline to serve. A custodian at any time may designate a trust company or an adult (other than the person who made the gift) as "successor custodian."

A custodian may resign at any time by delivering written notice to the minor (if she is at least fourteen years of age) and to the successor custodian. The resigning custodian must deliver the custodial property to the successor custodian. If a custodian dies or becomes incapacitated without having designated a successor, the Act contains rules for the appointment of a successor.

Legal Tip

Making gifts to minors is an important part of many estate plans. Whenever possible, the gifts should be made pursuant to the Arizona Uniform Transfers to Minors Act, as discussed above.

Guardianships

A guardian is a person appointed by the court to guard the health, safety, and welfare of another. A guardian may be appointed for a minor (anyone under the age of eighteen) or for an incapacitated person. The term "incapacitated person" is defined by law to mean any person who is impaired by reason of mental illness, mental deficiency, mental disorder, physical illness or disability, chronic use of drugs, chronic intoxication, or other cause, except minority, to the extent that he or she lacks sufficient understanding or capacity to make or communicate responsible decisions concerning himself or herself. The person for whom a guardian is appointed is called the "ward."

Generally speaking, a guardian has the same powers and authority over a ward that a parent has over a child. The guardian may, for instance, consent to medical treatment and other professional services for the ward. The guardian may also consent to psychiatric and psychological care. When it comes to the *property* of the ward, however, the guardian has very limited powers. If the ward has property in need of management or protection, a conservator should be appointed. A "conservator" is a person appointed to protect the property of a disabled person. (Conservatorships are discussed in the next chapter.) In some cases, the ward needs both a guardian and a conservator, which may or may not be the same person.

Guardian of a Minor

A parent of a minor can, by last will and testament, appoint a guardian for her. In order for this so-called testamentary appointment to become effective: (1) both parents must be dead or (2) the surviving parent's parental rights must have been terminated or (3) the surviving parent must be incapacitated. Otherwise, the surviving parent will have the care and custody of the child (even if the parents are divorced and the deceased parent was awarded sole custody). If the minor child is fourteen years of age or older, the child may object to the appointment of the guardian. If the child objects, the court will base the appointment on "the welfare and best interests of the minor."

The court may appoint a guardian for an unmarried minor if both parents are dead or their rights to custody have been terminated or suspended by circumstances or court order. Any person whose appointment would be in the best interests of the minor may be appointed. In most cases, this likely will be a relative of the minor. If the court appoints a guardian because the parents are unable or unwilling to care for their child, the guardianship may be terminated upon a change of those circumstances.

Guardian of an Incapacitated Person

A guardian for an incapacitated person may be appointed by will of a parent or spouse or by court order. Most often appointment is by court order. Court appointment of a guardian for an incapacitated person involves a judicial proceeding. Notice of the proceeding must be given to the person alleged to be incapacitated and to all other persons who have a legal interest in the outcome, such as a spouse, parents, and adult children. The court will hold a hearing on the issue of incapacity. To protect the rights of the alleged incapacitated person, the court will appoint an attorney to represent the person, an investigator to investigate the allegations concerning the person, and a physician to examine the person. The court will appoint a guardian only if it is satisfied, after considering all the evidence, that the person is incapacitated and in need of a guardian.

The court retains jurisdiction over all guardianship proceedings. The guardian is, thus, accountable to the court for all actions on behalf of the ward until the guardian's resignation, removal, or termination of appointment.

Conservatorships

A conservator is a person who acts as a trustee of another person's property. If a minor (a person under eighteen) or a disabled adult owns property that needs protection and management, a conservator should be appointed. The same person may serve as a conservator and guardian. (For a discussion concerning guardianships, please refer to the preceding chapter.)

A conservatorship proceeding may be started by an elderly person who desires protection of her property, or by any person interested in the estate, affairs, or welfare of the disabled person. The disability may be mental or physical. Missing persons and prisoners of war are considered disabled persons under the conservatorship statutes.

There is no requirement that an adult be declared "incompetent" in order for a conservator to be appointed. The test for disability is whether or not the adult is able to manage her property and affairs effectively. The court, depending on the nature of the alleged disability, may appoint a physician to examine the person and an investigator to investigate the issue of disability.

Once a conservatorship petition is filed, notice must be given to certain persons whose interests may be affected by the outcome of the proceeding. Those persons include a spouse, a guardian, parents, and children. Any interested person may participate in the proceeding and may file a demand for notice. If a demand for notice is filed, the person filing the demand will receive notice of all events and copies of all court papers in the proceeding.

In a conservatorship proceeding, the court *may* appoint an attorney to represent the minor and *must* appoint an attorney to represent the adult if she does not have counsel of her own. The appointment of counsel is to ensure that the alleged disabled person's rights are protected.

The conservator must furnish a bond to ensure the faithful performance of her duties. The court determines the amount of the bond based on the circumstances of each case, although the bond amount generally will be equal to the amount of the property plus one year's expected income (i.e., interest, dividends, and benefits). The conservator's bond is subject to periodic review, and the amount may be adjusted by the court from time to time. A conservator's bond may be purchased from most insurance companies.

The conservator is vested with legal title to all property of the protected person. The court-issued Letters of Conservatorship are evidence of the authority of the conservator. The conservator has the power to sell, buy, lease, transfer, encumber, or otherwise dispose of the property of the protected person. The exercise of these broad powers is subject to fiduciary duties and the same standard of care applicable to trustees. When in doubt regarding a particular transaction or course of action, the conservator may ask the court for instructions.

The conservator must file an inventory of the protected person's assets within ninety days after the conservator's appointment. The conservator must account to the court annually and also on termination. The accounts must contain details concerning all income and expenses during the accounting period, gains and losses on assets, and other information relating to the value of the estate. If the conservator is requesting attorney's fees be paid from the estate, a petition for approval of attorney's fees must also be filed.

A conservator may resign by petitioning the court or may be removed for good cause. If the conservator resigns, is removed, or dies, the court may appoint a successor conservator.

The conservatorship should terminate: (1) in the case of a minor, when the minor reaches age eighteen (assuming no other disability), (2) in the case of a disabled adult, when the disability has ceased, and (3) in all cases, when the protected person dies. Upon termination of the conservatorship, title to the assets passes to the person for whom the conservator was appointed or, if that person is deceased, to her estate.

Appendixes

Unified Credit Exemption Amounts

Gift and Estate Tax Table

CREDIT / EXCLUSION FOR ESTATE TAXES		
Year	**Applicable Credit**	**Applicable Exclusion***
2006–2008	$780,800	$2,000,000
2009	$1,455,800	$3,500,000
2010		Not applicable—estate tax repealed†
2011 and thereafter	$345,800	$1,000,000
CREDIT / EXCLUSION FOR GIFT TAXES		
2005 and thereafter	$345,800	$1,000,000

*   The exclusion is the amount that can be transferred without tax because of the credit.

†   Under current law, the estate tax is repealed for the year 2010 only.

APPENDIX B

Durable Health Care Power of Attorney

GENERAL INSTRUCTIONS: Use this Durable Health Care Power of Attorney form if you want to select a person to make future health care decisions for you so that if you become too ill or cannot make those decisions for yourself the person you choose and trust can make medical decisions for you. Talk to your family, friends, and others you trust about your choices. Also, it is a good idea to talk with professionals such as your doctor, clergyperson and a lawyer before you sign this form.

Be sure you understand the importance of this document. If you decide this is the form you want to use, complete the form. **Do not sign this form until** your witness or a Notary Public is present to witness the signing. There are further instructions for you about signing this form on page three.

1. Information about me: (I am called the "Principal")

My Name: _____   My Age: _____
My Address: _____   My Date of Birth: _____
_____   My Telephone: _____

2. Selection of my health care representative and alternate: (Also called an "agent" or "surrogate")

I choose the following person to act as my representative to make health care decisions for me:

Name: _____   Home Telephone: _____
Street Address: _____   Work Telephone: _____
City, State, Zip: _____   Cell Telephone: _____

I choose the following person to act as an alternate representative to make health care decisions for me if my first representative is unavailable, unwilling, or unable to make decisions for me:

Name: _____   Home Telephone: _____
Street Address: _____   Work Telephone: _____
City, State, Zip: _____   Cell Telephone: _____

3. What I AUTHORIZE if I am unable to make medical care decisions for myself:

I authorize my health care representative to make health care decisions for me when I cannot make or communicate my own health care decisions due to mental or physical illness, injury, disability, or incapacity. I want my representative to make all such decisions for me except those decisions that I have expressly stated in Part 4 below that I do not authorize him/her to make. If I am able to communicate in any manner, my representative should discuss my health care options with me. My representative should explain to me any choices he or she made if I am able to understand. This appointment is effective unless and until it is revoked by me or by an order of a court.

The types of health care decisions I authorize to be made on my behalf include but are not limited to the following:

> To consent or to refuse medical care, including diagnostic, surgical, or therapeutic procedures;
> To authorize the physicians, nurses, therapists, and other health care providers of his/her choice to provide care for me, and to obligate my resources or my estate to pay reasonable compensation for these services;
> To approve or deny my admittance to health care institutions, nursing homes, assisted living facilities, or other facilities or programs. By signing this form I understand that I allow my representative to make decisions about my mental health care except that generally speaking he or she cannot have me admitted to a structured treatment setting with 24-hour-a-day supervision and an intensive treatment program – called a "level one" behavioral health facility – using just this form;

Developed by the Office of Arizona Attorney General
TERRY GODDARD
www.azag.gov

1

Updated August 27, 2007
(All documents completed before August 27, 2007 are still valid)
DURABLE HEALTH CARE POWER OF ATTORNEY

DURABLE HEALTH CARE POWER OF ATTORNEY (Cont'd)

➤ To have access to and control over my medical records and to have the authority to discuss those records with health care providers.

4. DECISIONS I EXPRESSLY DO NOT AUTHORIZE my Representative to make for me:

I do not want my representative to make the following health care decisions for me (describe or write in "not applicable"):

_____

_____

_____

_____

5. My specific desires about autopsy:

> NOTE: Under Arizona law, an autopsy is not required unless the county medical examiner, the county attorney, or a superior court judge orders it to be performed. See the General Information document for more information about this topic. Initial or put a check mark by one of the following choices.

_____ Upon my death I DO NOT consent to (want) an autopsy.
_____ Upon my death I DO consent to (want) an autopsy.
_____ My representative may give or refuse consent for an autopsy.

6. My specific desires about organ donation: ("anatomical gift")

> NOTE: Under Arizona law, you may donate all or part of your body. If you do not make a choice, your representative or family can make the decision when you die. You may indicate which organs or tissues you want to donate and where you want them donated. Initial or put a check mark by A or B below. If you select B, continue with your choices.

_____ **A.** I DO NOT WANT to make an organ or tissue donation, and I do not want this donation authorized on my behalf by my representative or my family.
_____ **B.** I DO WANT to make an organ or tissue donation when I die. Here are my directions:

   1. What organs/tissues I choose to donate: (Select a or b below)
      _____ **a.** Any needed parts or organs.
      _____ **b.** These parts or organs:
         1.) _____
         2.) _____
         3.) _____

   2. What purposes I donate organs/tissues for: (Select a, b, or c below)
      _____ **a.** Any legally authorized purpose (transplantation, therapy, medical and dental evaluation and research, and/or advancement of medical and dental science).
      _____ **b.** Transplant or therapeutic purposes only.
      _____ **c.** Other: _____

   3. **What organization or person I want my parts or organs to go to:**
      _____ **a.** I have already signed a written agreement or donor card regarding organ and tissue donation with the following individual or institution: (Name) _____

      _____ **b.** I would like my tissues or organs to go to the following individual or institution: (Name) _____
      _____ **c.** I authorize my representative to make this decision.

Developed by the Office of Arizona Attorney General   Updated August 27, 2007
TERRY GODDARD   (All documents completed before August 27, 2007 are still valid)
www.azag.gov   2   DURABLE HEALTH CARE POWER OF ATTORNEY

DURABLE HEALTH CARE POWER OF ATTORNEY (Cont'd)

7. About a Living Will:

> NOTE: If you have a Living Will and a Durable Health Care Power of Attorney, **you must attach** the Living Will to this form. A Living Will form is available on the Attorney General (AG) web site. Initial or put a check mark by box A or B.

_____ **A.** I have SIGNED AND ATTACHED a completed Living Will in addition to this Durable Health Care Power of Attorney to state decisions I have made about end of life health care if I am unable to communicate or make my own decisions at that time.
       B. I have NOT SIGNED a Living Will.

8. About a Prehospital Medical Care Directive or Do Not Resuscitate Directive:

> NOTE: A form for the Prehospital Medical Care Directive or Do Not Resuscitate Directive is available on the AG Web site. Initial or put a check mark by box A or B.

_____ **A.** I and my doctor or health care provider HAVE SIGNED a Prehospital Medical Care Directive or Do Not Resuscitate Directive on paper with ORANGE background in the event that 911 or Emergency Medical Technicians or hospital emergency personnel are called and my heart or breathing has stopped.
_____ **B.** I have NOT SIGNED a Prehospital Medical Care Directive or Do Not Resuscitate Directive.

HIPPA WAIVER OF CONFIDENTIALITY FOR MY AGENT/REPRESENTATIVE

_____ **(Initial)** I intend for my agent to be treated as I would be with respect to my rights regarding the use and disclosure of my individually identifiable health information or other medical records. This release authority applies to any information governed by the Health Insurance Portability and Accountability Act of 1996 (aka HIPAA), 42 USC 1320d and 45 CFR 160-164.

SIGNATURE OR VERIFICATION

A. I am signing this Durable Health Care Power of Attorney as follows:

My Signature: _____ Date: _____

B. I am physically unable to sign this document, so a witness is verifying my desires as follows:

Witness Verification: I believe that this Durable Health Care Power of Attorney accurately expresses the wishes communicated to me by the principal of this document. He/she intends to adopt this Durable Health Care Power of Attorney at this time. He/she is physically unable to sign or mark this document at this time, and I verify that he/she directly indicated to me that the Durable Health Care Power of Attorney expresses his/her wishes and that he/she intends to adopt the Durable Health Care Power of Attorney at this time.

Witness Name (printed): _____
Signature: _____ Date: _____

SIGNATURE OF WITNESS OR NOTARY PUBLIC:

> NOTE: At least one adult witness OR a Notary Public must witness the signing of this document and then sign it. The witness or Notary Public CANNOT be anyone who is: (a) under the age of 18; (b) related to you by blood, adoption, or marriage; (c) entitled to any part of your estate; (d) appointed as your representative; or (e) involved in providing your health care at the time this form is signed.

Developed by the Office of Arizona Attorney General   Updated August 27, 2007
TERRY GODDARD   (All documents completed before August 27, 2007 are still valid)
WWW.AZAG.GOV   3   DURABLE HEALTH CARE POWER OF ATTORNEY

DURABLE HEALTH CARE POWER OF ATTORNEY (Last Page)

A. **Witness:** I certify that I witnessed the signing of this document by the Principal. The person who signed this Durable Health Care Power of Attorney appeared to be of sound mind and under no pressure to make specific choices or sign the document. I understand the requirements of being a witness and I confirm the following:

> ➤ I am not currently designated to make medical decisions for this person.
> ➤ I am not directly involved in administering health care to this person.
> ➤ I am not entitled to any portion of this person's estate upon his or her death under a will or by operation of law.
> ➤ I am not related to this person by blood, marriage or adoption.

Witness Name (printed): _____
Signature: _____ Date: _____
Address: _____

Notary Public (NOTE: If a witness signs your form, you DO NOT need a notary to sign):

STATE OF ARIZONA   ) ss
COUNTY OF _____)

The undersigned, being a Notary Public certified in Arizona, declares that the person making this Durable Health Care Power of Attorney has dated and signed or marked it in my presence and appears to me to be of sound mind and free from duress. I further declare I am not related to the person signing above by blood, marriage or adoption, or a person designated to make medical decisions on his/her behalf. I am not directly involved in providing health care to the person signing. I am not entitled to any part of his/her estate under a will now existing or by operation of law. In the event the person acknowledging this Durable Health Care Power of Attorney is physically unable to sign or mark this document, I verify that he/she directly indicated to me that this Durable Health Care Power of Attorney expresses his/her wishes and that he/she intends to adopt the Durable Health Care Power of Attorney at this time.

WITNESS MY HAND AND SEAL this ___ day of _____, 20___.
Notary Public _____ My Commission Expires: _____

OPTIONAL:
STATEMENT THAT YOU HAVE DISCUSSED
YOUR HEALTH CARE CHOICES FOR THE FUTURE
WITH YOUR PHYSICIAN

NOTE: Before deciding what health care you want for yourself, you may wish to ask your physician questions regarding treatment alternatives. This statement from your physician is not required by Arizona law. If you do speak with your physician, it is a good idea to have him or her complete this section. Ask your doctor to keep a copy of this form with your medical records.

On this date I reviewed this document with the Principal and discussed any questions regarding the probable medical consequences of the treatment choices provided above. I agree to comply with the provisions of this directive, and I will comply with the health care decisions made by the representative unless a decision violates my conscience. In such case I will promptly disclose my unwillingness to comply and will transfer or try to transfer patient care to another provider who is willing to act in accordance with the representative's direction.

Doctor Name (printed): _____
Signature: _____ Date: _____
Address: _____

Developed by the Office of Arizona Attorney General
TERRY GODDARD
www.azag.gov
                                        4
Updated August 27, 2007
(All documents completed before August 27, 2007 are still valid)
DURABLE HEALTH CARE POWER OF ATTORNEY

APPENDIX C

Prehospital Medical Care Directive

STATE OF ARIZONA
PREHOSPITAL MEDICAL CARE DIRECTIVE (DO NOT RESUSCITATE)
(IMPORTANT—THIS DOCUMENT MUST BE ON PAPER WITH ORANGE BACKGROUND)

GENERAL INFORMATION AND INSTRUCTIONS: A Prehospital Medical Care Directive is a document signed by you and your doctor that informs emergency medical technicians (EMTs) or hospital emergency personnel not to resuscitate you. Sometimes this is called a DNR – Do Not Resuscitate. If you have this form, EMTs and other emergency personnel will not use equipment, drugs, or devices to restart your heart or breathing, but they will not withhold medical interventions that are necessary to provide comfort care or to alleviate pain. IMPORTANT: Under Arizona law a Prehospital Medical Care Directive or DNR must be on letter sized paper or wallet sized paper on an orange background to be valid.

You can either attach a picture to this form, or complete the personal information. You must also complete the form and sign it in front of a witness. Your health care provider and your witness must sign this form.

1. **My Directive and My Signature:**

In the event of cardiac or respiratory arrest, I refuse any resuscitation measures including cardiac compression, endotracheal intubation and other advanced airway management, artificial ventilation, defibrillation, administration of advanced cardiac life support drugs and related emergency medical procedures.

Patient (Signature or Mark): _____   Date: _____

PROVIDE THE FOLLOWING INFORMATION:	**OR**	ATTACH RECENT PHOTOGRAPH HERE:
My Date of Birth _____ My Sex _____ My Race _____ My Eye Color _____ My Hair Color _____		**HERE**

2. **Information About My Doctor and Hospice** (if I am in Hospice):

Physician: _____   Telephone: _____

Hospice Program, if applicable (name): _____

3. **Signature of Doctor or Other Health Care Provider:**

I have explained this form and its consequences to the signer and obtained assurance that the signer understands that death may result from any refused care listed above.

Signature of Licensed Health Care Provider: _____   Date: _____

4. **Signature of Witness to My Directive:**

I was present when this form was signed (or marked). The patient then appeared to be of sound mind and free from duress.

Signature: _____   Date: _____

Developed by the Office of the Arizona Attorney General
TERRY GODDARD
www.azag.gov

Updated February 12, 2007
(All documents completed before February 12, 2007 are still valid)
PREHOSPITAL MEDICAL CARE DIRECTIVE (DNR)

APPENDIX D

Durable Mental Health Care Power of Attorney

STATE OF ARIZONA
DURABLE MENTAL HEALTH CARE POWER OF ATTORNEY
Instructions and Form

GENERAL INSTRUCTIONS: Use this Durable Mental Health Care Power of Attorney form if you want to appoint a person to make future mental health care decisions for you if you become incapable of making those decisions for yourself. The decision about whether you are incapable can only be made by an Arizona licensed psychiatrist or psychologist who will evaluate whether you can give informed consent. Be sure you understand the importance of this document. Talk to your family members, friends, and others you trust about your choices. Also, it is a good idea to talk with professionals such as your doctor, clergyperson, and a lawyer before you sign this form.

If you decide this is the form you want to use, complete the form. **Do not sign this form until** your witness or a Notary Public is present to witness the signing. There are more instructions about signing this form on page 3.

1. Information about me: (I am called the "Principal")

My Name: _____   My Age: _____
My Address: _____   My Date of Birth: _____
_____   My Telephone: _____

2. Selection of my health care representative and alternate: (Also called an "agent" or "surrogate")

I choose the following person to act as my representative to make mental health care decisions for me:

Name: _____   Home Telephone: _____
Street Address: _____   Work Telephone: _____
City, State, Zip: _____   Cell Telephone: _____

I choose the following person to act as an alternate representative to make mental health care decisions for me if my first representative is unavailable, unwilling, or unable to make decisions for me:

Name: _____   Home Telephone: _____
Street Address: _____   Work Telephone: _____
City, State, Zip: _____   Cell Telephone: _____

3. Mental health treatments that I AUTHORIZE if I am unable to make decisions for myself:

Here are the mental health treatments I authorize my mental health care representative to make on my behalf if I become incapable of making my own mental health care decisions due to mental or physical illness, injury, disability, or incapacity. If my wishes are not clear from this Durable Mental Health Care Power of Attorney or are not otherwise known to my representative, my representative will, in good faith, act in accordance with my best interests. This appointment is effective unless and until it is revoked by me or by an order of a court. My representative is authorized to do the following **which I have initialed or marked**:

_____ **A. About my records:** To receive information regarding mental health treatment that is proposed for me and to receive, review, and consent to disclosure of any of my medical records related to that treatment.
_____ **B. About medications:** To consent to the administration of any medications recommended by my treating physician.
_____ **C. About a structured treatment setting:** To admit me to a structured treatment setting with 24hour-a-day supervision and an intensive treatment program licensed by the Department of Health Services, which is called a "level one" behavioral health facility.
_____ **D. Other:** _____
_____
_____

Developed by the Office of Arizona Attorney General
TERRY GODDARD
www.azag.gov   1

Updated August 27, 2007
(All documents completed before August 27, 2007 are still valid)
DURABLE MENTAL HEALTH CARE POWER OF ATTORNEY

121

DURABLE MENTAL HEALTH CARE POWER OF ATTORNEY (Cont'd)

4. Durable Mental health treatments that I expressly DO NOT AUTHORIZE if I am unable to make decisions for myself: (Explain or write in "None")

_____
_____
_____

5. Revocability of this Durable Mental Health Care Power of Attorney: This Durable Mental Health Care Power of Attorney is made under Arizona law and continues in effect for all who rely upon it except those who have received oral or written notice of its revocation. Further, I want to be able to revoke this Durable Mental Health Care Power of Attorney as follows: (Initial or mark A or B.)

_____ **A.** This Durable Mental Health Care Power of Attorney is IRREVOCABLE if I am unable to give informed consent to mental health treatment.

B. This Durable Mental Health Care Power of Attorney is REVOCABLE at all times if I do any of the following:

1.) Make a written revocation of the Durable Mental Health Care Power of Attorney or a written statement to disqualify my representative or agent.
2.) Orally notify my representative or agent or a mental health care provider that I am revoking.
3.) Make a new Durable Mental Health Care Power of Attorney.
4.) Any other act that demonstrates my specific intent to revoke a Durable Mental Health Care Power of Attorney or to disqualify my agent.

6. Additional information about my mental health care treatment needs (consider including mental or physical health history, dietary requirements, religious concerns, people to notify and any other matters that you feel are important):

_____
_____
_____

HIPPA WAIVER OF CONFIDENTIALITY FOR MY AGENT/REPRESENTATIVE

_____ **(Initial)** I intend for my agent to be treated as I would be with respect to my rights regarding the use and disclosure of my individually identifiable health information or other medical records. This release authority applies to any information governed by the Health Insurance Portability and Accountability Act of 1996 (aka HIPAA), 42 USC 1320d and 45 CFR 160-164.

SIGNATURE OR VERIFICATION

A. I am signing this Durable Mental Health Care Power of Attorney as follows:

My Signature: _____ Date: _____

B. I am physically unable to sign this document, so a witness is verifying my desires as follows:

Witness Verification: I believe that this Durable Mental Health Care Power of Attorney accurately expresses the wishes communicated to me by the Principal of this document. He/she intends to adopt this Durable Mental Health Care Power of Attorney at this time. He/she is physically unable to sign or mark this document at this time. I verify that he/she directly indicated to me that the Durable Mental Health Care Power of Attorney expresses his/her wishes and that he/she intends to adopt the Durable Mental Health Care Power of Attorney at this time.

Witness Name (printed): _____

Signature: _____ Date: _____

Developed by the Office of Arizona Attorney General   Updated August 27, 2007
TERRY GODDARD   (All documents completed before August 27, 2007 are still valid)
www.azag.gov   2   DURABLE MENTAL HEALTH CARE POWER OF ATTORNEY

DURABLE MENTAL HEALTH CARE POWER OF ATTORNEY (Last Page)

SIGNATURE OF WITNESS OR NOTARY PUBLIC

NOTE: At least one adult witness OR a Notary Public must witness the signing of this document and then sign it. The witness or Notary Public CANNOT be anyone who is: (a) under the age of 18; (b) related to you by blood, adoption, or marriage; (c) entitled to any part of your estate; (d) appointed as your representative; or (e) involved in providing your health care at the time this document is signed.

A. Witness: I affirm that I personally know the person signing this Durable Mental Health Care Power of Attorney and that I witnessed the person sign or acknowledge the person's signature on this document in my presence. I further affirm that he/she appears to be of sound mind and not under duress, fraud, or undue influence. He/she is not related to me by blood, marriage, or adoption and is not a person for whom I directly provide care in a professional capacity. I have not been appointed as the representative to make medical decisions on his/her behalf.

Witness Name (printed): _____
Signature: _____ Date and time: _____
Address _____

B. Notary Public: (NOTE: If a witness signs your form, you DO NOT need a notary to sign)

STATE OF ARIZONA   ) ss
COUNTY OF   _____)

The undersigned, being a Notary Public certified in Arizona, declares that the person making this Durable Mental Health Care Power of Attorney has dated and signed or marked it in my presence and appears to me to be of sound mind and free from duress. I further declare I am not related to the person signing above, by blood, marriage or adoption, or a person designated to make medical decisions on his/her behalf. I am not directly involved in providing care as a professional to the person signing. I am not entitled to any part of his/her estate under a will now existing or by operation of law. In the event the person acknowledging this Durable Mental Health Care Power of Attorney is physically unable to sign or mark this document, I verify that he/she directly indicated to me that the Durable Mental Health Care Power of Attorney expresses his/her wishes and that he/she intends to adopt the Durable Mental Health Care Power of Attorney at this time.

WITNESS MY HAND AND SEAL this _____ day of _____, 20____.
Notary Public: _____ My commission expires: _____

OPTIONAL:
REPRESENTATIVE'S ACCEPTANCE OF APPOINTMENT

I accept this appointment and agree to serve as agent to make mental health treatment decisions for the Principal. I understand that I must act consistently with the wishes of the person I represent as expressed in this Durable Mental Health Care Power of Attorney or, if not expressed, as otherwise known by me. If I do not know the Principal's wishes, I have a duty to act in what I, in good faith, believe to be that person's best interests. I understand that this document gives me the authority to make decisions about mental health treatment only while that person has been determined to be incapacitated which means under Arizona law that a licensed psychiatrist or psychologist has the opinion that the Principal is unable to give informed consent.

Representative Name (printed): _____
Signature: _____ Date: _____

Developed by the Office of Arizona Attorney General
TERRY GODDARD
www.azag.gov   3   Updated August 27, 2007
(All documents completed before August 27, 2007 are still valid)
DURABLE MENTAL HEALTH CARE POWER OF ATTORNEY

APPENDIX E

Letter to My Personal Representative

STATE OF ARIZONA
LETTER TO MY REPRESENTATIVE(S)
About Powers of Attorney Forms and Responsibilities

To My Representative:
Name: _____
Address: _____
_____
_____

To My Alternate Representative:
Name: _____
Address: _____
_____
_____

A.   What I Ask You to Do For Me: Arizona law allows me to make certain medical and financial decisions as to what I want in the future if I become unable or incapable of making certain decisions for myself. I have completed the following document(s), and I want you to be my representative or alternate representative for the following purposes. (Initial or check one or more of the following):

_____   1.   Durable Health Care Power of Attorney
_____   2.   Durable Mental Health Care Power of Attorney

B.   Why I Named an Alternate Representative: I chose two representatives in case one of you is unable to act for me when the time arises. I ask that you accept my selection of you as my representative or alternate. If you do not return the Power of Attorney form(s) and this letter to me or inform me differently, I will assume that you have agreed to be my representative.

C.   Your Responsibilities as My Representative: By selecting you, I am saying that I want you to make some very important decisions for me about my future health care needs if I become unable to make these decisions for myself. I might need you to carry out my medical choices as indicated in the enclosed Powers of Attorney, even if you do not agree with them. Please read the copies of the Powers of Attorney I am giving you. This is a very serious responsibility to accept. You will be my voice and will make medical decisions on my behalf. Other than what I have indicated in the Powers of Attorney as to my specific directions on certain issues, I am trusting your judgment to make decisions that you believe to be in my best interests. If at any time you do not feel that you can undertake this responsibility for any reason, please let me know. If you are unsure about any of my directions, please discuss them with me. If you are not willing to serve as my representative, please tell me so I can choose someone else to help me.

As to Health Care: You are not financially responsible for paying my health care costs merely by accepting this responsibility. Under Arizona law, you are not liable for complying with my decisions as stated in the Powers of Attorney or in making other health care decisions for me if you act in good faith.

D.   What Else You Should Do: Please keep a copy of my Powers of Attorney and other documents in a safe place. Please read these documents carefully and discuss my choices with me at any time. I will give copies of my health care Powers of Attorney to my physician, and I will give copies of any or all of these Powers of Attorney to my family and any other representative I may choose. I authorize you to discuss with them the Powers of Attorney, including, as applicable, my medical situation, or any medical concerns about me. Please work with them and help them to act in accordance with my desires and in my best interests. I appreciate your support, and I thank you for your willingness to help me in this way.

Signature: _____   Date: _____

Printed Name: _____

Developed by the Office of the Arizona Attorney General
TERRY GODDARD
www.azag.gov

Updated February 12, 2007
(All documents completed before February 12, 2007 are still valid)
LETTER TO REPRESENTATIVE(S)

APPENDIX F

Living Will

STATE OF ARIZONA
LIVING WILL (End of Life Care)
Instructions and Form

GENERAL INSTRUCTIONS: Use this Living Will form to make decisions now about your medical care if you are ever in a terminal condition, a persistent vegetative state or an irreversible coma. You should talk to your doctor about what these terms mean. The Living Will states what choices you would have made for yourself if you were able to communicate. It is your written directions to your health care representative if you have one, your family, your physician, and any other person who might be in a position to make medical care decisions for you. Talk to your family members, friends, and others you trust about your choices. Also, it is a good idea to talk with professionals such as your doctor, clergyperson and a lawyer before you complete and sign this Living Will.

If you decide this is the form you want to use, complete the form. **Do not sign the Living Will until your witness or a Notary Public is present to watch you sign it.** There are further instructions for you about signing on page 2.

> **IMPORTANT: If you have a Living Will and a Durable Health Care Power of Attorney, you must attach the Living Will to the Durable Health Care Power of Attorney.**

1. **Information about me:** (I am called the "Principal")
   My Name: _____   My Age: _____
   My Address: _____   My Date of Birth: _____
   My Telephone: _____

2. **My decisions about End of Life Care:**

NOTE: Here are some general statements about choices you have as to health care you want at the end of your life. They are listed in the order provided by Arizona law. You can initial any combination of paragraphs A, B, C, and D. **If you initial Paragraph E, do not initial any other paragraphs.** Read all of the statements carefully before initialing to indicate your choice. You can also write your own statement concerning life-sustaining treatments and other matters relating to your health care at Section 3 of this form.

____ A. **Comfort Care Only:** If I have a terminal condition I do not want my life to be prolonged, and I do not want life-sustaining treatment, beyond comfort care, that would serve only to artificially delay the moment of my death. (NOTE: "Comfort care" means treatment in an attempt to protect and enhance the quality of life without artificially prolonging life.)

____ B. **Specific Limitations on Medical Treatments I Want:** (NOTE: Initial or mark one or more choices, talk to your doctor about your choices.) If I have a terminal condition, or am in an irreversible coma or a persistent vegetative state that my doctors reasonably believe to be irreversible or incurable, I do want the medical treatment necessary to provide care that would keep me comfortable, but I **do not** want the following:

   ____ 1.) Cardiopulmonary resuscitation, for example, the use of drugs, electric shock, and artificial breathing.
   ____ 2.) Artificially administered food and fluids.
   ____ 3.) To be taken to a hospital if it is at all avoidable.

____ C. **Pregnancy:** Regardless of any other directions I have given in this Living Will, if I am known to be pregnant I do not want life-sustaining treatment withheld or withdrawn if it is possible that the embryo/fetus will develop to the point of live birth with the continued application of life-sustaining treatment.

____ D. **Treatment Until My Medical Condition is Reasonably Known:** Regardless of the directions I have made in this Living Will, I do want the use of all medical care necessary to treat my condition until my doctors reasonably conclude that my condition is terminal or is irreversible and incurable, or I am in a persistent vegetative state.

____ E. **Direction to Prolong My Life:** I want my life to be prolonged to the greatest extent possible.

Developed by the Office of the Arizona Attorney General
TERRY GODDARD
www.azag.gov

Updated February 12, 2007
(All documents completed before February 12, 2007 are still valid)
1   LIVING WILL

STATE OF ARIZONA
LIVING WILL ("End of Life Care") (Cont'd)

3.   Other Statements Or Wishes I Want Followed For End of Life Care:

NOTE: You can attach additional provisions or limitations on medical care that have not been included in this Living Will form. Initial or put a check mark by box A or B below. Be sure to include the attachment if you check B.

_____**A.** I have not attached additional special provisions or limitations about End of Life Care I want.
_____**B.** I have attached additional special provisions or limitations about End of Life Care I want.

SIGNATURE OR VERIFICATION

A. I am signing this Living Will as follows:
My Signature: _____   Date: _____

B. I am physically unable to sign this Living Will, so a witness is verifying my desires as follows:

Witness Verification: I believe that this Living Will accurately expresses the wishes communicated to me by the principal of this document. He/she intends to adopt this Living Will at this time. He/she is physically unable to sign or mark this document at this time. I verify that he/she directly indicated to me that the Living Will expresses his/her wishes and that he/she intends to adopt the Living Will at this time.

Witness Name (printed): _____
Signature: _____   Date: _____

SIGNATURE OF WITNESS OR NOTARY PUBLIC

NOTE: At least one adult witness OR a Notary Public must witness you signing this document and then sign it. The witness or Notary Public CANNOT be anyone who is: (a) under the age of 18; (b) related to you by blood, adoption, or marriage, (c) entitled to any part of your estate; (d) appointed as your representative; or (e) involved in providing your health care at the time this document is signed.

A.   Witness: I certify that I witnessed the signing of this document by the Principal. The person who signed this Living Will appeared to be of sound mind and under no pressure to make specific choices or sign the document. I understand the requirements of being a witness. I confirm the following:
  • I am not currently designated to make medical decisions for this person.
  • I am not directly involved in administering health care to this person.
  • I am not entitled to any portion of this person's estate upon his or her death under a will or by operation of law.
  • I am not related to this person by blood, marriage, or adoption.

Witness Name (printed): _____
Signature: _____   Date: _____
Address:_____

B.   Notary Public: (NOTE: a Notary Public is only required if no witness signed above)

STATE OF ARIZONA   ) ss
COUNTY OF _____)

The undersigned, being a Notary Public certified in Arizona, declares that the person making this Living Will has dated and signed or marked it in my presence, and appears to me to be of sound mind and free from duress. I further declare I am not related to the person signing above, by blood, marriage or adoption, or a person designated to make medical decisions on his/her behalf. I am not directly involved in providing health care to the person signing. I am not entitled to any part of his/her estate under a will now existing or by operation of law. In the event the person acknowledging this Living Will is physically unable to sign or mark this document, I verify that he/she directly indicated to me that the Living Will expresses his/her wishes and that he/she intends to adopt the Living Will at this time.

WITNESS MY HAND AND SEAL this _____ day of _____, 20____.

Notary Public: _____   My commission expires: _____

Developed by the Office of the Arizona Attorney General   Updated February 12, 2007
TERRY GODDARD   (All documents completed before February 12, 2007 are still valid)
WWW.AZAG.GOV   2   LIVING WILL

APPENDIX G

Uniform Donor Card and Family Notification Form

Complete and keep in your wallet:

UNIFORM DONOR CARD

I,_____have spoken to my family about organ and tissue donation. The following people have witnessed my commitment to be a donor. I wish to donate the following:
☐ any needed organs and tissue
☐ only the following organs and tissues:_____

Donor Signature_____Date_____

Witness_____

Witness_____

Complete and give to your family:

FAMILY NOTIFICATION FORM

Dear_____
(family)

I would like to be an organ and tissue donor. I want you to know my decision because you will be consulted before donation can take place. I wish to donate the following:

☐ any needed organs and tissue
☐ only the following organs and tissues:

_____

Thank you for honoring my commitment to be an organ and tissue donor.

Donor Signature   Date

127

LaVergne, TN USA
17 August 2009
155048LV00001B/185/P